Policy and Practice in the Classroom

Series Editors
Richard Race
School of Education
University of Roehampton
London, United Kingdom

Barbara Read
School of Education
University of Glasgow
Glasgow, United Kingdom

Alaster Scott Douglas
School of Education
University of Roehampton
London, United Kingdom

This series will publish monographs exploring issues to do with education policy and practice in relation to classroom settings, with each book examining the implications of its research findings for educational policy and practice. Themes explored include teaching and learning; youth identities; inclusive education; education policy-making; de-schooling; student teachers; the primary classroom; and science teachers. If you have a proposal for the series you would like to discuss please contact: Eleanor Christie, eleanor.christie@palgrave.com

More information about this series at
http://www.springer.com/series/14548

Kate Hoskins

Youth Identities, Education and Employment

Exploring Post-16 and Post-18 Opportunities, Access and Policy

Kate Hoskins
School of Education
University of Roehampton
London, United Kingdom

Policy and Practice in the Classroom
ISBN 978-1-137-35291-0   ISBN 978-1-137-35292-7 (eBook)
DOI 10.1057/978-1-137-35292-7

Library of Congress Control Number: 2017940473

This Palgrave Macmillan imprint is published by Springer Nature
The registered company is Macmillan Publishers Ltd.
The registered company address is: The Campus, 4 Crinan Street, London, N1 9XW, United Kingdom

For my family: Damien, Zachary and Dylan

ACKNOWLEDGEMENTS

First and foremost, I would like to thank the Centre for Education Research in Equalities, Policy and Pedagogy (CEREPP) for funding the research project that informs this book. I would like to express my sincere gratitude to Professor Gill Crozier and Professor Penny Jane Burke for their support.

I would also like to thank my student and teacher participants at Parkfield School for their generosity in giving up their precious time to take part in my research. I am indebted to them.

Thanks also to Dr Barbara Read, Dr Alaster Douglas and Dr Richard Race for commissioning and reading drafts of this work. They have been incredibly patient and supportive throughout the process. Thanks also to Dr Sue Smedley who provided extremely useful comments on drafts of this work.

Finally, thanks must go to my family for their constant loving support. Sincere thanks to Damien, Zachary and Dylan. You are wonderful!

CONTENTS

LIST OF TABLES

CHAPTER 1

The Changing Landscape of Opportunity for Young People

At a recent family gathering, my 17-year-old nephew and I spent a lot of time talking about his plans for the coming year. His exams were looming, followed by an anxious wait for the results and important and economically loaded decisions about which higher education course to pursue. The pressure he was experiencing to make the grade was clear to all the family and no amount of time spent studying could relieve the strain, such was the weight of expectation. His experiences are not uncommon; according to research, pressure to achieve exam and university participation has become the norm for 17–18-year-olds (Hoskins and Barker 2014; Brown et al. 2011; Stobart 2008).

GRADUATION, GRADUATION, GRADUATION[1]

A review of graduate employment rates in England reflects the relative benefits experienced by graduates. According to the Labour Force Survey (2013) since 1992 the number of graduates has increased from 17% to 38%. In 1992 the graduate unemployment rate was 10% and in 2013 had fallen to 9%. The non-graduate unemployment rate was 13% in 1992 and had increased to just over 14% by 2013. Additionally, in 2013, the graduate employment rate stood at 87% and 'graduates were much more likely to work in high skill jobs than non-graduates' (Labour Force

© The Author(s) 2017
K. Hoskins, *Youth Identities, Education and Employment,*
Policy and Practice in the Classroom,
DOI 10.1057/978-1-137-35292-7_1

Survey 2013: 13). These figures illustrate the relative employment advantages experienced by graduates compared with non-graduates.

Indeed, in 2013 the Skills and Employment Survey found that degree-level jobs have overtaken jobs that require no formal qualifications (Coughlan 2013). But why has there been such an increase in graduate employment? Changes in the labour market, particularly the credentialisation of work, have played a central role in driving the expansion of higher education so that the volume of suitably skilled young people will match national and global workforce demands. Blue-collar,[2] white-collar and vocational jobs that might have required vocational qualifications in the 1980s and 1990s now require graduate educated employees, for example, administrative office workers, shop workers and childcare professionals (Ainley and Allen 2010). The increased pressure for young people to gain a degree has raised questions about who can study, where they can study and the sort of courses they should pursue to maximise their graduate employability potential.

Yet opportunities and outcomes for young people are unequal and complexly shaped by identity, geography and policy. Those from working-class backgrounds are still more likely to pursue blue-collar or vocational employment whilst middle-class young people tend to pursue white-collar or professional employment (Crozier et al. 2010). Gender still exerts a considerable impact on forms of work, working patterns and earning opportunities (Devine 2004; McDowell 2011). Ethnicity similarly influences education and employment possibilities and outcomes for many young people (Wadsworth et al. 2007). Thus, not all young people are equally positioned to access higher education or employment opportunities upon leaving school or further education aged 16, despite numerous widening participation policy initiatives aimed at improving inclusive education opportunities for all, but particularly non-traditional students.[3]

An additional pressure facing young people pursuing further and higher education is meeting the associated costs. The removal of the Educational Maintenance Allowance (EMA) for 16–17-year-olds in England has impacted on some young people's opportunities to participate in further education (McCrone et al. 2010). In terms of higher education, since 2010, undergraduates in England could expect to pay up to £9,000 in annual course tuition fees. Whilst not all degrees lead to commensurate salaries and employment status, all undergraduate degree courses cost approximately the same amount in annual tuition fees (Wilkins et al.

2013). The expectations for young people to take on high levels of personal debt from the age of 18 has contributed to the stress and pressure experienced by many.

THEMES OF THE BOOK

The social context influencing young people's post-16 choices is influenced by national education and employment policies alongside more individualised factors including social identity and family background. Thus, the central aims of this book are to investigate how policy, family background, social class, gender and ethnicity influence young people's post-16 and post-18 employment and education access and opportunities. I draw on existing literature alongside empirical data gathered for a small, qualitative semi-structured interview study with 22 young people in a case study state secondary school, to explore how policy changes to the financial arrangements for further and higher education and the changing youth employment landscape have impacted on young people's choices and pathways. I then explore how certain social identities provide some young people with the skills, knowledge and confidence required to navigate the current context of uncertainty and risk to achieve more secure education and employment outcomes. I investigate if/whether young people from more economically and culturally disadvantaged backgrounds are disproportionately affected by recent policy and economy changes. In Chapters 2 and 6 of the book, I provide comparative discussion of the influence of ongoing financial crises on young people located in other European Union countries – Greece and Spain – as these countries have experienced similar pressures on their further and higher education systems and have high levels of youth unemployment.

In the remainder of this introductory chapter I outline the economic, social and policy context of the book, introduce the empirical work underpinning the book and outline my theoretical and conceptual approach before finally outlining the chapters to follow.

ECONOMIC, SOCIAL AND POLICY CONTEXT

Since the spectacular failure of the financial markets in 2007 in the global north, austerity has been the maxim of governments around the world as they attempt to limit the effects of prolonged recession. Times are tough, particularly for young people considering higher education or seeking employment. In 2012, England's Conservative and Liberal Democrat Coalition government implemented several radical changes to the funding arrangements for further and higher education, which included cutting 'most ongoing direct public funding for tuition' (House of Commons Library 2016: 2) and increasing undergraduate university tuition fees from a maximum of £3,290 per annum to a maximum of £9,000 per annum. The government's intention was that fees over £6,000 would be the exception rather than the norm. However, the Office for Fair Access (OFFA) figures for 2012/13 indicate that '91 of 124 universities with access agreements will charge £9,000 for at least one course, and 42 will charge this figure as standard' (Office for Fair Access (OFFA) 2014: 1). Despite significant earning differences between forms of work, all undergraduate courses cost approximately the same.

Owing to the Coalition government's decision in 2010 to remove the £30 per week EMA in England available to teenagers from low-income families (defined as those families earning less than £30,810 p.a.), it became more expensive to participate in further education between the age of 16 and 18. Although contentious because of the differing views about the equity of EMA allocation and concerns about how the money was spent by some young people (McCrone et al. 2010), the EMA did give the opportunity for many young people from disadvantaged backgrounds to participate in further education (Chowdry et al. 2008). These changes to the funding available for further and higher education were deemed necessary by the Coalition government because of the wider context of fiscal contraction as a consequence of the global recession of 2008/2009 and the repercussions of this period of extreme austerity (Dorling 2014).

Policy changes to the financial structures underpinning further and higher education are not the only consequence of the global recession. Youth unemployment reached record highs in the period since 2007 across much of Europe and America and has contributed to a period of intense uncertainty for young people (Dorling 2014). In England, the Office for National Statistics (ONS) (2010: 1 in Elliott 2010: 1) figures show that

> the number of 16- to 24-year-olds out of work increased by 28,000 to 9,43,000, one of the highest figures since records began in 1992, giving a youth jobless rate of 19.8%.

Even those with degree-level qualifications have encountered problems with obtaining graduate employment; in 2010/11, the graduate employment rate in England was 62% (HESA, Higher Education Statistics Agency (HESA) 2012: 1). The ONS (2012: 5 in Osborne 2012: 1) reported that the rate of unemployment for new graduates in England was 18.9% in the final quarter of 2011. Although this figure is down from 20.7% in early 2010, it is more than four times the number for those graduating in 2004–2005. This unemployment rate has contributed to a situation in England where '25% of 21-year-olds who left university with a degree in 2011 were unemployed compared with 26% of 16-year-olds with GCSEs' (Osborne 2012: 1).

Similarly, in Spain, the global recession has had a significant impact on youth unemployment and it reached 50% among 15–29-year-olds during the spring of 2013 (Buck 2014). It is difficult to disaggregate the graduate and non-graduate unemployment rates in Spain, but at present, the youth unemployment rate in Spain is closer to 55% and rising (Buck 2014). Indeed, the youth unemployment rate in Spain is currently only second in the European Union to Greece, which recently reported that 62.9% of its young people were out of work (Burgen 2013).

In England, Spain and Greece, high youth unemployment has raised questions about the market value of a degree for securing employment in some sectors of the economy. The graduate employment rate raises questions about the viability of higher education, particularly in the generally less economically rewarding disciplines of social science, arts and humanities. In the current highly competitive employment market the intrinsic value of participating in education is impacted by the costs associated with gaining a degree. This issue is explored more fully in Chapter 5.

THE EMPIRICAL STUDY

Alongside reviewing existing research exploring youth employment and education possibilities and opportunities in England, Spain and Greece, I carried out qualitative research in one case study state school, which I have renamed Parkfield School. The inclusion of empirical data has enabled me to explore how young peoples' identities influence their post-16 and post-18 choices and pathways in complex and situated ways. The research involved semi-structured focus groups with 22 young people, aged between 15 and 16 years. The following research questions guided the content and focus of the semi-structured interviews:

1. How have aspects of the participants' gender, social class and ethnicity influenced their decisions about their post-16 and post-18 pathways?
2. How are the participants' choices and experiences influenced by the impact of cuts to EMA and the increase in university tuition fees?
3. How are the participants' plans for their post-16 and post-18 pathways influenced by the current employment context?
4. How does the research cohort decide upon their post-16 and post-18 pathways given the resources and support available to them from their parents and teachers?

The themes of the book are addressed through analysis and discussion of this empirical research alongside existing research. I also draw on Bourdieu's (1977) theoretical framework of habitus and field and Berger and Luckmann (1966) theory of social constructionism, to analyse and make sense of the young people's stories about their post-16 plans.

In what follows, I briefly summarise the study design to provide context and background information for the reader. The empirical research data presented in the book was collected for a Centre for Educational Research in Equalities, Policy and Pedagogy (CEREPP)-funded research project at the University of Roehampton. In 2012–2013 I conducted in-depth semi-structured focus groups with a group of 22 15–16-year-old students from varied social-class and minority-ethnic backgrounds in one case study co-educational state secondary academy school. The students were identified with the help of the Head of Post-16 Study, who was fully briefed on the aims of the project and the requirement for a diverse sample in terms of social identity. The Head of Post 16 Study was aware that the research aimed to explore the impact that changes to the financial arrangements for further and higher education and widespread youth unemployment have had on a small group of young people as they embark on their post-16 pathways.

The Head of Post 16 Study assisted me with locating potential participants for the study through a combination of purposive and convenience sampling. Flyers were put up in the sixth form common room requesting that potential participants contact me to express their interest. From the 42 young people who were interested in taking part in the project, I selected 22 with the help of the Head of Post 16 Study who was aware of the class, ethnic and gender balance I was hoping to achieve. However, despite these best efforts to construct a purposive sample, which included extensive email and telephone correspondence to confirm the dates and times for the focus groups, on the day, there were 18 girls and 4 boys. The gender skew was a result of several boys being unavailable at the last minute because of change in timetable for a big sporting tournament. I was unable to rearrange the date due to imminent examinations. The challenges of constructing a diverse sample highlighted the problematic nature of field research where even the best and most secure plans can be disrupted by the demands of a school's priorities.

The demographics of the locality in terms of population are typical for the selected London suburb and reflect some of the diversity of the city in social class and ethnicity terms. The suburbs of London, or outer London as they are sometimes referred to, are geographically quite different from inner London. The suburbs tend to have more space in terms of housing, outside community spaces such as parks and woodland, and more spacious town centres (Watt 2009). There is less traffic in the suburbs of London compared with central London, lower rates of crime and fewer concentrations of economic and social disadvantage (Watt 2009).

The 22 participants who participated in the case study are from varied social class and minority-ethnic backgrounds. The following table provides summary demographic information about the participants (Table 1.1):

Despite the initial challenges and changes, the sample has provided diversity in terms of class, gender and ethnicity to yield data that reflects a range of perspectives and helped me to explore how social class, gender and ethnicity have shaped the participants' future plans.

I selected the case study school carefully. I wanted to locate an 'ordinary' school, that is a school in the middle of the league tables,[4] although I was aware of how problematic this would be to achieve. As Maguire et al. (Maguire et al. 2011: 14) note 'it is possible to identify schools and for schools to be identified as "ordinary". But no school can possibly embrace this description for itself' in performative times. The school is located in a leafy London suburb that encompasses a diverse range of ethnic and social class groups. The school's Office for Standards in Education (Ofsted) report describes it as good with some outstanding features, and the A*-C GCSE[5] pass rate tends to be around 75/76% and with the high-status subjects of mathematics and English included the pass rate is around 56/57%. The free school meals

Table 1.1 Student participant demographic table

Pseudonym and focus group	Social class background (as articulated by participants)	Gender	Ethnicity	Planned next steps	Course at university
Ann – focus group 3	Working class	Female	Black African-Caribbean	University	Clinical Psychology
Claire – focus group 2	Working class	Female	White Irish	University	Not specified
Georgia – focus group 1	Working class	Female	White British	Unsure	N/A
Jen – focus group 5	Working class/middle class	Female	White British	University	Sociology
Jodie – focus group 3	Working class	Female	White British	University	Teaching
Kim – focus group 4	Working class	Female	Chinese	University	English language Teacher
Paul – focus group 5	Working class/middle class	Male	White British	University	Not specified
Sian – focus group 1	Working class	Female	White British	Unsure, potentially employment	N/A
Adele – focus group 3	Middle class	Female	Black African-Caribbean	University	Medicine
Adrian – focus group 4	Middle class	Male	White British	Russell Group university	Maths
Beth – focus group 4	Middle class	Female	White British	Russell Group university	Psychology
Claudia – focus group 4	Middle class	Female	White British	Russell Group university	Anthropology

Gemma – focus group 1	Middle class	Female	White British	University	Childhood studies
Julie – focus group 2	Middle class	Female	White British	University	Teaching
Laura – focus group 3	Middle class	Female	White British	University	Teaching
Paresh – focus group 3	Middle class	Female	Indian	University	Sociology
Sandra – focus group 1	Middle class	Female	White British	University	Sociology/ Teaching
Stephanie – focus group 1	Middle class	Female	White British	Unsure, probably employment	N/A
Susie – focus group 2	Middle class	Female	White British	University	Social work
Tim – focus group 4	Middle class	Male	White British	Russell Group university	Biochemistry
Jamal – focus group 2	Unsure	Male	Pakistani	University	Probably economics
Holly – focus group 2	Unsure/probably middle class	Female	White British	Unsure, maybe University but highly unlikely	N/A

(FSM)[6] rate is 14.8% compared with the borough[7] average of 18.6%, so the uptake is in the lower band. The school prioritises academic post-16 pathways with 21 A-level subjects and just one BTEC on offer. The school has recently gained academy[8] status, although the Head Teacher told me that he had felt pressurised to convert to benefit from the financial incentives associated with being an academy school in England.

Turning now to the project design, I decided to take a singular case study approach, where the school is taken as the 'bounded unit' of analysis and to gather 'rich data' using interviews and focus groups to explore the complex and situated experiences of the participants (Hamilton and Corbett-Whittier 2013: 11). I used a theory seeking and theory-testing case study, with the intention of producing 'a fuzzy generalisation – or proposition – which shows how the discovery may apply more widely' (Bassey 1999: 47). The strength of case studies comes from their attention to the subtlety and complexity of the case in its own right. I acknowledge that single case studies may 'limit what generalizations you are able to make' (Beare et al. 1989: 14) but argue that such research provides 'access to events or groups that are otherwise inaccessible to scientific investigation' (Yin 1994: 88).

The data was gathered during two intense, but short, periods of time with a six-month gap between the first and the second focus groups with the participants. I have used the case study approach to uncover some of the situated impacts of recent further and higher policy change as they are experienced by a small, diverse group of students, to explore how social identity and policy shapes young people's choices and pathways (Yin 1994).

The research complied with the ethical protocols set out by the University of Roehampton's code of practice and requirements; the British Education Research Association (BERA) (British Educational Research Association (BERA) 2011) revised ethical guidelines and the British Sociological Association (BSA) (2002) ethical guidelines.

I used a qualitative methodology and method to gather the participants' views. I conducted in-depth semi-structured, audio-recorded focus groups, which lasted approximately 1 hour, with 22 15–16-year-old students. The students were mainly interviewed in focus groups of 5. I had hoped all the focus groups would have four or five participants; however, because of timing issues on the fieldwork days, there was one group with two participants. The audio recordings were fully transcribed and analysed. Data coding was thematic and followed the Strauss and Corbin's

Table 1.2   Teacher participant demographic table

Name	Job title	Gender	Ethnicity
Chloe	Year 12/Post-16 Teacher	Female	White British
Emily	Head of Post-16 Study Sociology	Female	White British
Julia	Year 12/Post-16 Teacher	Female	White Irish
Maria	Year 12/Post-16 Teacher	Female	White British
Daniel	Year 12/Post-16 Teacher	Male	White British
Jasper	Year 12/Post-16 Teacher	Male	White British
John	Head of Post-16 Study	Male	White British

(Strauss and Corbin 1990: 61) approach of open coding where the aim is to 'break down, examine, compare, conceptualise and categorise data'. The coding process was followed by the construction of thematic categories related to addressing my research questions.

The focus groups explored the participants' plans and aspirations for their post-16 pathways. I asked them about whether they intended to apply for further and higher education or employment. They were asked to explain the motivations and factors informing their plans for the future and I particularly probed the role of the school and the role of the family in shaping and influencing these plans. The focus groups benefited from 'interaction found in a group' (Morgan 1988: 12), which was particularly useful for facilitating my attempt to 'stimulate people in making explicit their views, perceptions, motives and reasons' (Punch 2009: 147). Thus, the semi-structured focus groups disrupted, to some extent, the power dynamics within the research process, as the participants had opportunities to define and direct some of the information they chose to share.

Finally, I also carried out eight in-depth semi-structured interviews with teachers and senior leaders in the school. The semi-structured nature of the interviews was useful for gathering rich, detailed and descriptive data. The teachers also provided further insights into the factors informing the participants' plans for the future (Table 1.2).

THEORETICAL FRAMEWORK

To understand and analyse the participants' stories, I used Bourdieu's (1977) theory of habitus, field and cultural capital to frame the project design and data analysis. I utilised a social constructionist approach to the data collection and analysis to problematise constructions of gender in my participants' experiences, for example, any gendered educational pathways and career aspirations. Finally, I make reference to Putnam's (2000) theory of social capital to understand the role of bonding and bridging capital. This blend of theory enabled me to explore the tensions between structure and agency in the data.

Habitus refers to 'a system of durable, transposable dispositions which functions as the generative basis of structured, objectively unified practices' (Bourdieu and Passeron 1977, vii). The term characterises the recurring patterns of social class, social mobility and class fractions – that is the beliefs, values, conduct, speech, dress and manners – that are inculcated by everyday experiences within the family, particularly in early childhood (Mills 2008). These classed patterns are formed of individual and shared group dispositions.

The dispositions (capacities, tendencies, propensities or inclinations) that constitute habitus are acquired through a gradual process of inculcation in early childhood and thus habitus is a complex formulation of past and present (Hoskins and Barker 2014). The dispositions that individuals acquire are also structured in the sense that they reflect the social conditions within which they were acquired. An individual brought up in a working-class family, for instance, will have acquired dispositions which are different in certain respects from those acquired by individuals who were brought up in a middle-class family (Thomas 2001). The process of exploring habitus can illuminate a family's 'durable dispositions' and it is the dispositions that an individual acquires via familial socialisation that become, according to Bourdieu (1977) embodied, acting as markers, or signifiers, of the habitus, which can in turn illuminate an individual's social class location.

Bourdieu's (1977) concept of habitus provides a useful framework for interpreting the impacts of different 'fields', including familial, school and higher education institutions on the individual (see, e.g., Reay et al. 2010). Habitus is dynamic and interconnected to the field. A field consists of 'a set of objective, historical relations between positions anchored in certain forms of power (or capital)' (Bourdieu and Wacquant 1992: 227). Exploring how field and habitus influence young people's choices is useful as it enabled me to theorise how the fields of my participants' family and school shaped their pathways, sometimes providing them with an alternative course of action which moves them beyond the 'practical sense that inclines agents to act and react in specific situations' (Bourdieu 1993: 5).

Drawing on the work of Reay et al. (Reay et al. 2010: 116) I examine the process of reconciliation 'of the disjuncture between working-class background and academic dispositions'.

The natural familiarity of the schooling system experienced by some young people contrasts with the persistent disconnect experienced by many others. These differences according to Bourdieu (1977) relate to the alignment, or not, of habitus and field between an individual and the school, an alignment made possible by the possession of reified and valued dispositions and forms of cultural capital. It is knowledge of the unconscious codes underpinning the education system, which facilitates space for shared values between the individual and the social structure of schooling. Bourdieu (1977) has argued that the culture of the dominant group – that is, the group that controls the economic, social and political resources – is embodied in schools. Educational institutions ensure the profitability of the cultural capital of the dominant group, attesting to their gifts and merits. Educational differences are frequently misrecognised as resulting from individual giftedness rather than from class-based, structural differences. This ignores the ways that the abilities measured by scholastic criteria often stem not from natural 'gifts' but from 'the greater or lesser affinity between class cultural habits and the demands of the educational system or the criteria which define success within it' (Bourdieu and Passeron 1977, 22). Exploring the participants' habitus is a significant way to understand the different family backgrounds, values and beliefs they have experienced.

Despite its uses, habitus is a widely contested concept (James 2015; Reay 2004; Hey 2003; Nash 1999; Tooley and Darby 1998) and there are limitations involved with deploying habitus theory. In earlier work (Hoskins and Barker 2016) we identified three key criticisms, but there are others. The first criticism is the extent to which habitus is agentic as opposed to structural and deterministic. Mills argues that 'it is ironic that habitus has been subject to widespread criticism on the basis of its latent determinism' (Mills 2008: 80). However, it remains the case that a recurring criticism of habitus is its perceived potential for determinism (Calhoun et al. 1993). I have chosen to follow Nash (1999: 76), who asserts that 'habitus provides the grounds for agency, within a limited arena of choice, and thus is a theoretical escape from structuralist determinism'. As such, throughout this book I provide an agentic reading of habitus where individuals were able to transform their lives.

Second, 'habitus theory cannot satisfactorily account for anomalies in choice making processes reported by participants whose stories are not straightforward examples of social reproduction' (Hoskins and Barker 2016: 6). For this reason, I decided to adopt a multi-theoretical approach to this research that not only drew on habitus, but also the concepts of cultural capital and social constructionism, to provide a detailed and critical analysis of why and how young people make choices about their lives.

The final limitation relates to Bourdieu's fluid definitions of his key concepts, for example, the term 'dispositions'. As Jenkins (1992: 76) notes, dispositions 'might be no more than "attitudes", and indeed have often been understood as such'; thus, using habitus is problematised by the variants of definitions deployed (James 2015). I have attempted to address the slippage in definitions by providing clearly articulated and exemplified descriptions of habitus, field and cultural capital and drawing on these descriptions in the data analysis process. Whilst there are key limitations associated with drawing on habitus theory, it is arguably sufficiently useful in allowing me to explore and offer discussion of the impact it has had in my respondents' education pathways.

I have also used Berger and Luckmann (1966) theoretical concept of social constructionism to understand how the young people construct and maintain particular versions of their gender, class and ethnic identities. I have used social constructionism as the methodological approach to gathering and analysing the data, following the key tenets of the theory, as highlighted by Burr (2003: 2–4). Burr contends that social constructionism requires 'a critical stance toward taken-for-granted knowledge', that is, to problematise and critique the familiar. Second, Burr argues that there is the need to acknowledge 'historical and cultural specificity'. Third, Burr states it is important to take the view that 'knowledge is sustained by social processes'. Social scientists need to problematise and take a critical stance towards the socially constructed nature of, for example, the interview process. Fourth, 'knowledge and social action go together' – that is, knowledge can enable social change and change is a key aspect of the feminist project, which is a key aspect of my approach.

Utilising a social constructionist approach has allowed me to explore the influence of gender in my participants' perceptions and experiences of school and, for example, the gendered nature of their subject choices and career aspirations. Taking a social constructionist approach also enabled me to be self-reflexive and question the data I have gathered; nothing was taken as objective and this allowed me to bring a level of criticality to the data analysis and meaning-making process. Such an approach enabled me to use the results of the data to undermine assumptions about the world, for example, the idea that a person's success is only down to individual factors rather than structural and identity factors.

Finally, I make reference to social capital theory to understand how the participants draw on bonding and bridging capital to assist with their post-16 choices (Putnam 2000). According to Coleman (1994: 300) social capital is inherent 'in family relations and in community social organisations'. Putnam (1995: 66 in Phillips 2010: 493) identifies social capital as 'the features of social life networks, norms and trust' and highlights the importance of the reciprocal relationships existing within networks. In a subsequent work, he identifies two aspects of social capital, namely its potential for bonding and bridging (Putnam 2000). Bonding networks entail close ties with friends and family and provide support, whereas bridging networks have weaker ties, but are outward-looking and include contacts from diverse social backgrounds. In this research, bonding and bridging capital (Putnam 2000) are recognised together with the importance of close relationships within networks, as evident in Coleman's attention to the social capital provided by family relations where the close relationship between parent and child has the potential to influence a child's educational achievement (Coleman 1988). In using Putnam's definition I am drawing on a conservative and communitarian way of conceptualising social capital. However, despite this potential limitation, I have found bonding and bridging capital of value to explore if and how those participants seeking employment rather than university at age 18 benefit from access to bonding and bridging networks.

RESEARCHING IDENTITY

One aim of this book is to examine the influence of aspects of identity on the participants' post-16 decision-making process. The aspects of identity I focus on are social class, gender and ethnicity. In what follows, each of these is discussed.

There is much evidence that has consistently shown young people from a working-class background are more likely to end up in lower status employment compared with their typically more educationally successful middle-class peers (Gewirtz 2001; Archer et al. 2007; Allen 2014;

Mendick et al. 2015). Professional, managerial and skilled occupations and careers are typically the preserve of the middle classes whilst service, vocational, semi-skilled and unskilled forms of employment remain the domain of many of the working class (Hoskins and Barker 2014). The educationally successful working-class student disrupts such generalisations, but these discrepant cases are often little more than that. Indeed, they can be understood in Reay's (1997: 20) terms as 'the tokenistic edge of elitist policies', which legitimate policy makers' focus on individualistic outcomes for all, where structural inequality pales into insignificance when held up to the transformative power of individual agency.

Ethnicity has similarly been shown to have a determining effect on individuals from particular minority ethnic backgrounds. These effects are articulated in terms of racial stereotypes such as the hard working, academic south Asian student (Francis et al. 2010), the less able and less academic African-Caribbean student (Mirza 2009) and the compliant, shy and marginalised Indian and Pakistani student (Archer et al. 2010). These stereotypes have powerful consequences in terms of the ways that policy makers, educators, families and young people are positioned and position themselves in relation to educational, economic and employment possibilities for their future lives. The impact of ethnicity on the individual is keenly felt (Mirza 2009) yet arguably can seem to be overlooked or ignored amidst discourses that emphasise zero tolerance to racial abuse. That very zero tolerance approach to racism can silence discussions on lingering racialised inequalities experienced by minority ethnic groups and thus reinforce the regimes and effects of inequality, prejudice and social injustice. It is important, therefore, to have the language/discourses to talk about ethnicity (and gender and social class for that matter) in ways that are constructive rather than leaving people open to accusations of prejudice.

Gender has also been shown to have durable and demarcated effects on many young people's educational achievement from an early age (Skelton and Francis 2009). Francis (2000) has shown that gender has consequences on the subject choices young people make, the forms of assessment they prefer and the sort of career pathway they decide to follow. Others have similarly found that young people have a strong sense of their educational gender identity and this guides their choices and pathways (see, e.g., Leatz 1993; Acker 1994; Arnot 2008). Whilst there are disruptions to this somewhat essentialising projection, these again are few and are more likely to be experienced by a young person who has a more privileged class and ethnic identity. Despite numerous reforms and policy initiatives in the UK as elsewhere, for example, Women into Science and Mathematics (WISE), and drives to get more boys to read (Weiner 1985), gender positions and subject choices remain entrenched as binary and are repeatedly taken up and maintained in this way across all levels of schooling and education, from early childhood through to adulthood.

Taken together and drawing on an intersectional approach (Brah and Phoenix 2004), these aspects of identity form complex subjectivities and positions from which young people attempt to navigate their education and make plans for the future. An intersectional approach towards understanding identity is useful and opens up spaces to move beyond one-dimensional forms of analysis. But analysing and theorising the operation of intersectional identity is also a complex, contradictory, ambiguous and often unsatisfactory process. For example, how can a young woman, from a marginalised 'deficit' minority ethnic background with limited economic capital, disrupt powerful external positioning to achieve educational and later economic success? What would success for her look like? How could her success be replicated through social and educational policy to form a strategic and more widespread approach to challenging the power of identity stereotypes to formulate different, more successful outcomes? To provide an intersectional analysis, I take the view that identities are complicated, contradictory, culturally imbued, politically and economically inflected, and historically specific. Exploring an individual's identity reveals how social class, gender and ethnicity overlap, conflict and merge, creating, at particular moments, situated and contextualised intersections. Identities are not fixed; they alter over time, and in different spaces, as people construct and reconstruct their social realities resulting from the complex interplay between opportunity and experience. Hall (1990: 222) contends that:

> Identities are not as transparent and unproblematic as we think. Perhaps instead of thinking of identity as an already accomplished fact, which the new cultural practices then represent, we should think, instead, of identity as a production, which is never complete, always in process.

Viewing identity as a production and process that is changing, unstable, incomplete and fragmentary has enabled me to examine the relationships between class, gender and ethnicity in the participants' stories and in my analysis of literature exploring youth access and outcomes in education and employment. Analysing the intersections between class, gender and ethnicity has provided an understanding of the participants' educational experiences and how the nuances of their identity has shaped their pathways.

I draw on the framework of intersectionality to consider the historical specificity of multiple axes of differentiations and the effects of the intertwined nature of different strands of identity. I adopt the approach that the intersections between class, gender and race 'are simultaneously subjective, structural and about social positioning and everyday practices' (Brah and Phoenix 2004: 75). In taking this approach, I aim to illustrate the complexity of class, gender and ethnicity, as they appear in the participants' discussions of their plans for their education and employment and in relation to the literature discussed in Chapter 2.

Overview of Chapters

The chapters of the book are structured to reflect the research process. I begin by taking the reader through the theoretical and research process before presenting the data analysis. The chapters are structured as follows:

Chapter 2 – The Changing Context of Further and Higher Education and Youth Employment

Chapter 2 examines two areas of policy change: first, the impact of cuts to EMA; second, the impact of the increase in university tuition fees. Chapter 2 compares the university top-up policy in England to the higher education fee situation in Greece and Spain to explore the parallels of these countries with the English context. The chapter also considers the current youth employment context facing the participants and again makes links to Greece and Spain, as these countries are all experiencing high levels of youth unemployment (Nölke 2016; McCann 2010).

Chapter 3 – Post-16 Educational Choices and Decision-Making: Opportunities and Challenges

Chapter 3 explores how recent policy changes to further education policy (detailed in Chapter 2) have influenced young people's decisions about their post-16 pathways. The chapter also investigates how social class, gender and ethnicity have influenced the participants' post-16 decisions for their next steps. The chapter draws on the concepts of habitus and field to explore how the participants' family backgrounds along with their social identity have influenced their dispositions to choose particular pathways.

Chapter 4 – Post-18 Educational Choices: 'Our Students Need to Avoid the easyJet Version of Universities'

Chapter 4 investigates how recent policy changes to higher education tuition fees have influenced the students' views on attending university and provides the teachers' views on university as an option for their students. The chapter also explores how the students' gender, social class and ethnicity influences their decisions about attending university and the type of university course they intend to apply for.

Chapter 5 – Alternative Possibilities and Pathways: Youth Employment and Apprenticeships in a Graduate World

Chapter 5 considers some of the challenges and constraints facing those participants seeking employment rather than higher education at the age of 18. Chapter 5 explores the resources the participants have, to overcome the challenges of finding semi-skilled and skilled work and considers the assistance and support provided by their teachers, the school (Lanning and Rudiger 2012) and their families (Ball 2003) as well as their own resilience (Stein 2005).

Chapter 6 – The Contemporary Context of Youth Participation and Identities: Towards Challenging the Status Quo

The final chapter draws together the policy, theoretical and empirical insights set out in the book and I argue that post-16 educational pathways are shaped by the policy context and the participants' social class, gender and ethnicity. Thus, identities are argued to be a key predictor for understanding the participants' choices. The chapter summarises the further and higher education policy comparative analysis between England, Greece and Spain in relation to university top-up fees and employment outcomes. The chapter argues that the policy context in combination with the participants' identities produces particular historical possibilities and constraints. The chapter concludes by recommending policy changes which could assist young people, both in

England and the wider European context, to be better prepared, equipped and supported for educational and employment success, and help them to achieve their future ambitions.

CONCLUDING REMARKS

In this introductory chapter I have provided a rationale for the focus of the book to contextualise the key aims within existing literature on youth education and employment possibilities and opportunities and in relation to a qualitative research project that sought to understand and interpret 22 young people's plans for their post-16 pathways. I have also made inferences and comparisons with the youth employment context of Spain and Greece to show the similarities and differences related to the social and economic context in these countries. Despite government rhetoric in England, Spain and Greece about their commitment to educational and employment equality for all, inequality in opportunity and outcome, rooted in individual young people's ability to navigate social policy and social identity, are still the defining influences that shape young people's aspirations and achievements. I will be exploring these issues throughout the chapters that follow.

NOTES

1. Prior to election in 1997, Tony Blair, the leader of New Labour, stated that his three priorities if his party was elected was 'education, education, education'. In practice, the drive to increase participation in higher education in England has resulted in pressure for all young people to gain graduate qualifications.
2. The terms 'blue collar' and 'white collar' are occupational classifications that distinguish workers who perform manual labour from workers who perform professional jobs. Historically, blue-collar workers wore uniforms, usually blue, and worked in trade occupations. White-collar workers typically wore white, button-down shirts and worked in office settings. Other aspects that distinguish blue-collar and white-collar workers include earnings and education level.
3. In this book, I use the term non-traditional students to encompass school leavers, mature students, and other historically excluded groups, such as women, the working classes and those from minority ethnic backgrounds (Crozier et al. 2010).

4. Every year the government publishes data on the attainment of pupils in schools in England, in what it describes as 'achievement and attainment tables'.

5. GCSE refers to General Certificate in Secondary Education examinations, which students take at age 15-16 years in England.

6. Free school meals are available to children whose parent/carer is in receipt of state benefits.

7. London is formed of 32 boroughs, each with their own local politicians and governance structures.

8. Academy schools were introduced from 2000 onwards in England. They are state schools that are outside of Local Education Authority (LEA) control.

CHAPTER 2

The Changing Context of Further and Higher Education and Youth Employment

INTRODUCTION

This chapter begins with a discussion of neoliberalism to highlight how this concept has increasingly underpinned and influenced the social context throughout the United Kingdom and globally since the end of World War II (Jones 2015). I then discuss two key policy changes, arising, in part, from neoliberal discourses and ideology: first, the impact of cuts to the EMA; second, the impact of the increase in university top-up fees for tuition. I will be comparing the university fees top-up policy in England to the higher education fee situation in Greece and Spain to explore the parallels of these countries with the English context. Then finally, the chapter considers the current youth un/employment context facing young people in England and compares and contrasts this with youth un/employment in Greece and Spain (Nölke 2016; McCann 2010).

Throughout this chapter I argue that changes to further and higher education policy have increased the socio-economic gap between advantaged and disadvantaged young people. I contend that the influence of neoliberalism has been central to the restructuring within education and the economy and that certain social identities are better placed than others to manage these changes whilst maintaining an advantaged position. England, like many countries within the global north, has used the financial crisis in 2007 as a mandate to enact sweeping welfare and educational reforms, and this has reshaped the landscape facing young people as they

© The Author(s) 2017
K. Hoskins, *Youth Identities, Education and Employment,*
Policy and Practice in the Classroom,
DOI 10.1057/978-1-137-35292-7_2

navigate their way from compulsory to post compulsory education and the free market. The literature used throughout the chapter reveals the extent to which opportunities are bound up in time, place and space and inflected by the changing policy context.

THE CHANGING POLICY CONTEXT IN ENGLAND: THE INFLUENCE OF NEOLIBERALISM

Neoliberalism has been central to the changing higher education policy context in England since the 1970s. Ideas about neoliberalism have changed considerably since its widespread, global implementation in the 1970s (Harvey 2005). The British government's turn to neoliberalism was largely an attempt to restore economic power to a small, global elite (Harvey 2005). The economic decay of the 1970s, resulting from the problems with 'embedded liberalism' – referring to state intervention 'in industrial policy' and the creation of standards 'for the social wage by constructing a variety of welfare systems', including health and education – meant that an alternative capitalist system was required to avoid widespread movement towards socialism and even communism (Harvey 2005: 19). Neoliberalism revived stagnating economies around the world, although it was implemented and enacted differently in different contexts, for example through a coup in Chile, military takeover in Argentina and privatisation of state services in Mexico.

The global implementation of what Ong (2007: 4) calls 'big N neoliberalism', that is neoliberalism which is 'viewed as a dominant structural condition that projects totalizing social change', across a nation was achieved by the circulation of powerful ideological discourses advocating the value of freedom to democratic societies, through the construction of consent arising from 'common-sense' views of the economy and where necessary, through use of force (military and financial) (Harvey 2005). The net result has been global movement towards neoliberalism that reaches across all levels of social and economic life in the global north and south.

The ideology and effects of neoliberalism are apparent throughout the various arms of the state, including education. The first three decades after World War II were marked by increased state intervention in the provision of compulsory education for 5–15-year-olds and then from the 1970s for 5–16-year-olds. The ideology behind this provision determined that the welfare state would not only educate but also protect the housing provision and health of the population in interventionist ways. But from the late 1970s onwards, this state provision began to slowly decline and was replaced by neoliberal policies and ideologies that, broadly speaking, advocated free trade, deregulation, privatisation and economic liberalism (Adams 2001). Harvey (2005: 2) provides a useful definition of neoliberal ideology, which I have drawn on in this book:

> Neoliberalism is in the first instance a theory of political economic practices that proposes that human well-being can best be advanced by liberating individual entrepreneurial freedoms and skills within an institutional frame-work characterized by strong private property rights, free markets and free trade. The role of the state is to create and preserve an institutional frame-work appropriate to such practices [...] Furthermore, if markets do not exist (in areas such as land, water, education, health care, social security, or environmental pollution) then they must be created, by state action if necessary. But beyond these tasks the state should not venture. State inter-ventions in markets (once created) must be kept to a bare minimum because, according to the theory, the state cannot possibly possess enough information to second-guess market signals (prices) and because powerful interest groups will inevitably distort and bias state interventions (particu-larly in democracies) for their own benefit. (Harvey 2005: 2)

To follow this viewpoint, the application of these neoliberal principles to compulsory and post-compulsory education has resulted in quasi-markets opening up within education that create competition between schools, colleges and universities. The creation of competition in education is premised on the political belief that competition is good and raises stan-dards and that parents need to be able to exercise choice about where to send their children to be educated (Ball 2012, 2016). The consequences of these neoliberal education policies have been far reaching, particularly in relation to the delivery, provision and financial arrangements for both further and higher education, highlighted below.

NEOLIBERALISM AND FURTHER EDUCATION: CUTS TO FINANCIAL SUPPORT

To encourage young people, particularly those from economically and socially disadvantaged backgrounds, to continue with their studies, the New Labour government (1997–2009) introduced the Education

Maintenance Allowance (EMA) in 2004 in England. The EMA was piloted in England in September 1999 following recommendations set out in a report by the Social Exclusion Unit (SEU 1999) entitled Bridging the Gap. Allocation of EMA money was based on annual household income. The policy was banded as follows:

> Students from families earning up to £20,817 receive £30 a week, those with incomes between £20,818 and £25,521 receive £20 a week, while those with household incomes of £25,522 and £30,810 receive £10 a week. (BBC News, 2011, accessed 10 August 2015)

Between 2004 and 2010, families were means tested and allocated funds for their 16–17-year-olds to pursue further education on the basis of monthly income. The EMA was credited with providing economic support for economically disadvantaged young people to continue with their education beyond the age of 16. The New Labour government argued that EMA was an effective mechanism for improving the participation and completion rates within all subject areas of further education.

Although New Labour asserted that EMA succeeded at increasing participation in further education amongst disadvantaged young people, a report by researchers at the National Foundation for Education Research (NFER) revealed that there has been much debate about the effectiveness and efficiency of the policy (McCrone et al. 2010). At the centre of the debate are issues relating to the cost effectiveness, impact and efficiency of the programme, which was contested by the incoming Coalition government in 2010 who argued that EMA was

> expensive and wasteful, costing over £560 m a year with administration costs amounting to £36 m – at a time when ministers are trying to reduce the national deficit. (BBC News, 2011 accessed August 2015)

The Department for Education argued that '90% of students who receive EMA would still continue with their education without the payment' (BBC News, 2011, accessed 10 August 2015). The evidence of considerable uptake of further education regardless of state supplied financial support provided the government with a mandate to discontinue EMA, despite the positive outcomes the policy had in enabling disadvantaged students to continue with their studies. The Institute for Fiscal Studies (IFS) claimed that even if there was 90% take-up of further education by students regardless of the financial support leading to 'deadweight costs', these costs are offset by the benefits of getting young people into training (Chowdry and Emerson 2010).

Prior to the election, the Conservative and Liberal Democrat parties had stated that they were committed to continuing with EMA to assist disadvantaged students with their further education. However the Education Secretary between 2010 and 2014, Michael Gove, abolished the EMA allowance soon after taking office on the basis that it was a 'bad policy and it was axed in favour of a smaller "targeted bursary" for the very poorest students' (The Telegraph 2012, accessed August 2015). The targeted bursary introduced by Gove represented a significant decrease in financial support for many 16–19–year-olds from low-income families, who no longer qualified for financial assistance with their further education.

Despite being discontinued, there is evidence to suggest that EMA did increase participation and engagement in further education amongst disadvantaged young people (Chowdry and Emerson 2010). The removal of EMA had a 'hugely detrimental impact according to University and Colleges Admissions Services (UCAS) figures with 56,000 fewer students staying on in the last academic year' (Peever 2013). A quantitative review after the first year of implementation suggested that participation in further education as a result of EMA had increased by 'around 5.9% percentage points' (Ashworth et al. 2001: 133). Chowdry and Emerson (2010: 1) draw on the research they conducted for the Institute for Fiscal Studies (IFS), to argue that the economic effectiveness of EMA impacted positively on those staying in education beyond the age of 16:

> In particular, it (EMA) increased the proportion of eligible 16-year-olds staying in education from 65% to 69%, and increased the proportion of eligible 17-year-olds in education from 54% to 61%.

Research by Chowdry et al. (2008) indicated that EMA did successfully increase participation in further education by between 5 and 6% consistently throughout the duration of the initiative. This consistent increase in participation and completion was considered by New Labour to be enough of a return to warrant the continuation of the programme (Chowdry et al. 2008).

Archer et al. (2010) conducted research in urban schools with disadvantaged young people and asked participants for their views on EMA. The majority of their participants did not like the idea of EMA as they viewed it as 'basically bribing kids to stay on in school' (Archer et al. 2010: 117). The general consensus amongst these participants was that if a young person was committed to pursuing further education they would do so regardless of any financial incentive. Thus, Archer et al. (2010) concluded that in their research findings, the EMA was constructed as a negative policy that sought to reward the undeserving poor. A further finding related to the working-class young men in their study who typically contrasted earning with learning and the EMA sat awkwardly within this formulation.

Following Harvey's (2005) construction of neoliberalism, I argue that EMA can be viewed as a neoliberal policy as it focused on encouraging and regulating the participation in further education of working-class young people, in a 'directive way' (Archer et al. 2010: 116). EMA extended the arm of the state into disadvantaged young people's lives and compelled and coerced them into participation in further education through extrinsic, neoliberal financial incentives rather than through intrinsically rewarding policy approaches such as engaged participation, which is constructed and delivered as an inclusive approach to gaining knowledge. Rather than address and dismantle some of the structural inequalities such as low-waged employment that result in some young people and their families finding that they are unable to meet the costs of further education – particularly for those in rural locations – the government took a financial add-on and controlling approach to addressing this educational inequality. Such an approach, although beneficial to some young people, will not radically alter or challenge the neoliberal principles, which underpin and shape further education in England.

NEOLIBERALISM AND HIGHER EDUCATION: UNIVERSITY TUITION FEES

Changes to the provision and funding of higher education have always been closely linked to changes in the English economy. Since the late 1970s the provision of compulsory and post-compulsory education in England has been subjected to the forces of neoliberalism in a variety of ways. The management of school, college and university budgets, the delivery of staff development and training and curriculum content are just some of the areas that have radically altered. The turn to neoliberalism in education is linked to the wider social and political context, where successive British governments have sought ways to address the shortcomings of economic growth by increasing competition between education providers. The argument here is that if competition increases, overall standards will improve within education, which will enable England to improve its position in international education league tables, for example the Programme for International Student Assessment (PISA). Governments construct an improved standing in the international education league tables as a marker of a country's economic potential and status in the global context.

Turning now to higher education, it is apparent that this sector has similarly been subject to various forms of neoliberalism and has undergone rapid and intense changes since the 1970s. Government funding of university students rapidly declined in the 1970s and 1980s and student undergraduate tuition fees were introduced – first for overseas students but by the 1990s this was extended to home students (discussed below). The introduction of the 'new public management' (NPM) approach in the 1990s altered the internal and external organisational structure and operation of universities (Rhodes 1994). Radice (2013: 412–413) describes the internal and external changes enacted as a result of NPM:

> Internally, NPM centred on devolved budgetary systems and a shift in focus from academic goals and processes to financial management. Although practices varied a good deal, the central feature for most academics was that the subject department or school became a 'cost centre'. In this approach, all costs and revenues of the university as a whole are attributed to individual cost centres; the department must cover its salary costs, and its allocated share of central costs such as physical facilities, library, IT services and central administration, from the income attributable to its teaching, research and other commercial activities.

Universities had moved from a system of free higher education to charging fees for higher education because of significant reductions in government funding (Davis et al. 2012). Universities increasingly buy in a range of support from private companies including catering services, maintenance services and plagiarism software to name just a few. Buying in services can be problematic in terms of the efficiency and cost effectiveness of the services. These changes to higher education have raised myriad ethical questions about the purpose of education, the delivery of education and access to education (Deem et al. 2007).

Increasing university tuition fees is arguably an example of the impact that neoliberalism has had on higher education. The 1997 Dearing Report was commissioned to investigate:

> How the purposes, shape, structure, size and funding of higher education, including support for students, should develop to meet the needs of the United Kingdom over the next 20 years. (Dearing 1997: 1)

The report recommended that higher education in the future needed to be funded by a mixture of government grants and the introduction of student paid tuition fees to a maximum sum of £1000. In 1998 the decision was taken by the New Labour government to introduce university tuition fees in England. The Teaching and Higher Education Act 1998 legislated for £1000 tuition fees to be charged. From 1998, universities needed to generate their own income to remain economically viable (Deem et al. 2007). Those universities who could not fill the funding gap would either have to reduce their provision or risk closure. Such changes signalled an emphasis change in the culture of universities.

By 2004, the maximum amount a student paid towards tuition fees had increased to £3000 through new legislation implemented as part of the 2004 Higher Education Act. In 2009, the tuition fees increased again to £3290, leading to the establishment of the 2009 Browne Review into Higher Education. The results of the Browne Review were published in 2010 and recommended that university tuition fees increase to a maximum of £9000 per annum. Despite widespread protest against the proposals from students, parents and academics, the Coalition government went ahead with a House of Commons vote on 9 December 2010. The result of the vote was a slim majority (323 for and 302 against) and the maximum cap for university tuition fees was increased to £9,000.

The literature suggests that initially, the introduction of tuition fees and subsequent increases would deter and discourage disadvantaged students from pursuing higher education (Archer and Hutchings 2000; Callender 2003; Callender and Jackson 2008). These studies suggested that introduction of tuition fees would exclude non-traditional students from participation in higher education. Archer and Hutchings (2000) conducted 14 focus groups with 109 working-class students located in London to understand their perceptions of higher education. The sample included male and female students aged between 16 and 30 years of age, who were not currently participating in higher education. Archer and Hutchings (2000: 569) found that their participants acknowledged the potential economic, social and self-development benefits higher education could provide, but also viewed it as 'inherently risky, demanding great investment and costs and yielding uncertain returns'. Thus the participants' perceptions of debt were an important issue in determining whether they would apply for higher education or not.

Callender's (2003: 8) study also found that attitudes towards debt were an important factor in potential students' decisions to undertake higher education:

> Prospective students with tolerant attitudes towards debt were one and quarter times more likely to go to university than those who were debt averse, all other things being equal. Debt aversion deterred entry into HE but was also a social class issue. Those most anti-debt are the focus of widening participation policies and include those from the lowest social classes.

Callender (2003) noted that in addition to those from a working-class background, lone parents, Muslims, Pakistanis, black and minority ethnic groups also tended to be more debt averse than their middle-class male counterparts. Types of secondary school attended also influenced views about debt with those students from independent schools more comfortable with taking on debt and the associated risks due to the assumed financial security within the family (Callender 2003).

A later study showed that those students who were debt averse were still more likely to attend university than those who were anti-debt (Callender and Jackson 2008). However, debt aversion was shown to influence the length of course taken by students with many seeking to reduce the time they spend in higher education to reduce the build-up of debt. The study also revealed that those working-class students pursuing higher education would deploy debt avoidance strategies such as living at home, to reduce the costs of their education (Callender and Jackson 2008), thus highlighting the disparity in choice available to young people from different social backgrounds.

In research by Davies et al. (2008) 1,628 16–18-year-old students located across 20 schools/further education colleges were surveyed about their decision-making processes to participate in higher education.

A further 37 students took part in qualitative interviews to further explore and understand how they would decide which university to attend. The key finding of this research is that 'finance affects the likelihood of participation in higher education' (Davies et al. 2008: 1). Indeed, two thirds of their sample had cited debt as a factor that had impacted on their decision-making 'much' or 'very much' (Davies et al. 2008: 27). The study also supported Callender and Jackson (2008) findings that those students from lone parent, Muslim and minority ethnic groups were more likely to be debt averse than their (white) middle-class, male and independent school peers.

However, research by Dunnet et al. (2012) challenged some of the findings of the earlier research cited above and showed that course and university reputation mattered more to potential students than paying tuition fees. The research did find that parental prior engagement with higher education also mattered and that students who did not have first-hand familial experience of university were marginally more affected by tuition fee increases. The study also found that students from working-class families were more likely to choose to attend a university closer to home to reduce some of the living expenses associated with studying away.

More recently research carried out by Wilkins et al. (2013) surveyed 1,549 Year 12 students from four institutions spread across England. The research found that financial concerns were a key factor in the choice to participate or not to participate in higher education. Specifically, they found that students displayed anxiety about taking on debt and consequently considered a diverse range of universities and potential courses both in England and abroad. But despite a slight dip in application numbers following the increase in tuitions fees, applications have subsequently increased. This increase is partly due to students' awareness of the need for a degree to undertake professional work, as well as many forms of white-collar and some forms of blue-collar work (Wilkins et al. 2013). The fear of being left behind or missing out on opportunities has resulted in non-traditional students opting for those institutions that are located nearer to their homes.

Although the tuition fee cap has been set at £9000, universities have been encouraged by the government to charge less than the maximum amount. However, over the past few years since the higher fees were increased, the majority of universities in England have charged the full fee amount, mainly because of reputational factors as relatively cheap courses may be perceived to lack quality, and also due to funding deficits created by the removal of much of the government financial support for the sector. As Bowl and Hughes have argued (2014: 17):

> In the current policy context in English higher education, universities have a legitimate interest in their own viability and they may need to secure this through the adoption of different strategic responses to changing policy pressures.

In the market-led, neoliberal formulation of higher education where universities are structured as for-profit businesses that can now fail and fold, many institutions have needed to charge the maximum amount of undergraduate and postgraduate fees to remain financially viable.

The subtle yet persistent infiltration of neoliberal policies and practices in higher education has raised social justice questions about the sorts of young (and older) people who can access higher education and the sorts of identities valued by many universities – that is, white and middle class. Recent research suggests that there are some shared characteristics evident in potential undergraduate students according to their attitudes towards debt, and the type of institution they apply to attend (Bradley and Ingram 2013). These different students present different sorts of economic opportunities to higher education institutions (Davies et al. 2008; Bradley et al. 2013). Despite the widening participation agenda (discussed in the following section), which aimed to increase participation in higher education, it remains the case that middle-class, white young people still dominate the elite, 'old'[1] Russell Group universities and working-class and minority ethnic young people dominate the 'new' universities (Burke 2013, 2012; Reay et al. 2010). The widening participation agenda has not managed to penetrate deeply embedded social differences between advantaged and disadvantaged groups and has arguably consolidated a two-tier higher education system between the middle and the working classes.

THE WIDENING HIGHER EDUCATION PARTICIPATION AGENDA

These rapid changes to the funding arrangements for higher education were impacted by the drive to widen participation in higher education. In 1997, New Labour 'set a target for 50 per cent of the under-30s population to have participated in HE by 2010' (Medway et al. 2003: 7).

The widening participation policy agenda was influenced by the government's need to provide a labour force for the developing 'knowledge economy'. The Economic Social Research Council (ESRC) understand the term knowledge economy to refer to:

> the economic structure emerging in the global information society in which economic success increasingly depends on the effective utilisation of intangible assets such as knowledge, skills and innovative potential. (cited in Roberts 2009: 285)

The need to be knowledgeable can be viewed as a response to the rapidly changing forms of employment in the twenty-first century, partly as a result of the digital media age, the effects of neoliberal education policy and globalisation.

To meet this changing employment and economic landscape, widening participation in higher education (and indeed further education) was deemed necessary by the UK government. Levy and Hopkins (2010: 6) make the case for the graduates to support the 2020 knowledge economy and the economic competitiveness of the United Kingdom, arguing that the 'structural change in the economy is creating a strong and increasing need for more highly educated workers'. Thus, the increased provision of forms of higher education was

> based on the belief that a nation's economic competitiveness can be enhanced if a greater proportion of its population gain the kinds of knowledge, skills and understanding fostered by higher education and a social justice rationale where the concern is to extend the benefits of higher education beyond a middle-class elite. (Woodrow et al. 1998: 8)

The Former Secretary of State for Education, David Blunkett, explicitly stated that 'world class higher education ensures that countries can grow and sustain high-skill businesses, and attract and retain the most highly-skilled people' (Blunkett 2008). This has led to significant expansion of all sectors of higher education over the past 15 years, with some disciplines with low unemployment rates – such as medicine and teaching – undergoing extensive expansion as larger numbers of graduates seek more assured and secure employment outcomes (HESA, Higher Education Statistics Agency (HESA) 2012).

One consequence of neoliberal forces and the demands of government to constantly 'up skill' the workforce is the reality that young people leaving school today have become part of a global 'degree generation' (Bradley et al. 2013). There is widespread acknowledgement that further education followed by a degree has become the minimum necessary currency for almost all entry-level professional jobs and is therefore considered compulsory for the majority of middle-class students and increasing numbers of working-class students (Reay et al. 2005; Hoskins and Barker 2014).

In terms of the individual, the economic rationale for participating in some form of higher education is perhaps more sharply visible today than at any point in the recent past. Currently, a young person attending a prestigious 'old' university in England has a higher chance of obtaining a professional or managerial-level job and of attaining higher earnings in the future than someone graduating with the same qualification from a less prestigious 'new' university (Chevalier and Conlon 2003; Bratti et al. 2004; Power and Whitty 2006; Hussein et al. 2009). There are also significant differences in the salaries graduates from different degree courses can expect to attain, with some study programmes (e.g. Law, Economics, Engineering) consistently resulting in better earning outcomes for graduates than other degrees, for example, those in arts and humanities and the social sciences (O'Leary and Sloane 2005; Walker and Zhu 2011).

Yet despite the economic pressure to graduate, Lauder et al. (2010) have shown that the economic value of degrees varies significantly in terms of the sorts of returns students can expect once they join the employment market. They found that the top end of the employment scale, which includes professional occupations, has seen an increase in the wage distribution, whereas at the bottom end of the salary spectrum, wages have sharply decreased (Lauder et al. 2010). This reduction in the economic returns from a degree (Lauder et al. 2010) raises questions about the value of gaining a degree. In a trend identified in America during the 1960s and 1970s, the predominance of those with graduate qualifications led to an overqualified workforce with too few jobs at the top (Bowles and Gintis 1976).

However, any concerns about the costs of higher education, economic and emotional, seem to be superseded by the economic and employment imperatives to be educated to at least undergraduate level. Thus graduation, graduation, graduation appears to be the political and economic message to young people making choices about what they are going to do with their lives once they have left school.

HIGHER EDUCATION TUITION FEES: THE SITUATION IN GREECE AND SPAIN

An aim of this book is to provide comparative discussion of the influence of the ongoing financial crisis on young people's identity and choice making processes at age 16 and 18 in two other European Union countries – Greece and Spain – as these countries have experienced similar pressures on their further and higher education systems and high levels of youth unemployment. Comparisons can shed light on the English context. Therefore in this section I now explore the context and recent changes influencing higher education structure, provision and delivery in Greece.

The global recession of 2007 has further reshaped the economic context of much of the global north, particularly Europe. At the time of writing, Greece had been recently facing 'Grexit', that is an exit from membership to the Eurozone, due to defaulting on a repayment as a result of significant levels of national debt. The ongoing financial crisis in Greece has had wide-ranging implications in addition to specific impact on the structure and delivery of higher education, particularly in terms of extending and entrenching neoliberal policies and practices: for example, the increase in competition between higher education institutions to recruit students and orientate courses to maximise student employability. Yet Zmas (2014) argues that politicians have used the crisis as a rationale for extending the reach of neoliberal organisational approaches to higher education provision. Zmas (2014) contends that neoliberal market forces have been a growing influence on higher education provision for over 40 years, since the 1974 fall of the military junta and the subsequent democratisation of the state.

Two recent changes to the governance and quality assurance systems underpinning higher education in Greece occurred in 2005 and 2007. In 2005 the Parliamentary Act No 3374/2005 was passed and the Greek higher education system was subject to legal requirements for:

> the construction of indicators reflecting the quality of HE provision and the implementation of continuous assessment of the universities and the TEIs, both through internal (i.e. self-evaluation) and external procedures (evaluation by outsider experts). (Gouvias 2012: 70)

This strengthening of quality assurance systems and processes was in line with the Bologna process, with its emphasis on improving the

harmonisation of governance, quality and accountability in higher education provision across Europe. The new rules on quality assurance were,
according to Gouvias (2012: 70) 'reinforced in 2007 when it [sic] passed
through the Greek Parliament Bill that created a new operating framework
for HE institutions'. The 2007 framework emphasised quality assurance
improvements through changes to study patterns, reduced financial
autonomy for universities and changes to staff and student assessment
structures (Gouvias 2012).

The emphasis on improved quality assurance processes has required
Greek universities to 'neoliberalise' their professional practice. Zmas
(2014: 496) summarises the neoliberalisation as follows:

> The changes under consideration include new forms of governance, the
> merger of appropriate institutions, a squeeze on public funding, tighter
> financial controls and a strict review of management structures within the
> university sector more broadly.

Yet despite the increase in 'big N neoliberalisation' of many aspects of
higher education in Greece (Ong 2006), universities, in contrast to
England, do not charge fees to home and European undergraduate students and only small fees are payable by international students.
Postgraduate courses including masters and doctoral courses are subject
to minimal fee requirements of up to 1500 Euros per year. However, the
absence of fees for higher education masks some of the hidden costs of
Greek education – such as widespread attendance at private secondary
schools to prepare middle-class students for university entrance examinations. According to Marseilles (2010), in practice, Greece offers 'an
expensive free education' (http://www.universityworldnews.com/arti
cle.php?story=2010012409184186, accessed 16 November 2015), due
to the hidden costs of private education deemed necessary by many middle-class families to protect the economic privilege of future generations.

The Organization for Economic Cooperation and Development's
(OECD) (2011) report entitled 'Strong Performers and Successful
Reformers in Education: Education Policy Advice for Greece' is scathing
in its assessment of higher education provision in Greece, citing a crisis of
values, outdated policies and inadequate organisation structures as just
some of the key problems. The report also recommended that student
numbers were reduced by over 10,000 students 2011–2012, and suggested that the issue of higher education costs needed to be revisited.

Since 2007, the Greek state has experienced increasing control and autonomy over university finances and can make decisions about how budgets are allocated. Thus the national and international economic pressure experienced by Greece since the banking crisis in 2006 has required the state to rethink its policy priorities and to attempt to find a balance between educating its future workforce and managing the impact of public sector funding cuts.

Turning now to Spain, it is apparent that during the last 10 years, it has experienced similar financial pressures to Greece and England. As the financial crisis of 2007 rippled across the global north, Spain is 'among the group of European countries hardest hit by the economic crisis' (Banyuls and Recio 2012: 199). The reasons for Spain's financial vulnerability in the 2007 crisis rest on three key factors: the downturn in construction and resultant increase in family indebtedness, the significant decline in manufacturing and production (accelerated by entry to the European Union), and the expansion of the public sector (Banyuls and Recio 2012). The creation and expansion of a public sector within Spain has resulted in a 'contradictory attempt to apply neoliberal policies in a society that was trying to develop a   previously non-existent – welfare state' (Banyuls and Recio 2012: 200). This contradiction, between implementing neoliberal financial and education policies and a simultaneous attempt to construct an extended welfare state, has impacted on the structure and delivery of higher education across Spain.

Yet, costs for higher education in Spain have remained comparatively minimal despite the economic pressure. Public universities, which include the most prestigious institutions, charge their undergraduates annual registration fees of between €500 and €1120 and tuition fees of up to €1200. Yet as Aguilera-Barchet (2012) points out, the actual cost to the state for each student is approximately tenfold the costs to students and stands at €10,000 on average, per student. In contrast, private universities charge between €5000 and €12,000 for the registration fee alone per year. In the private university sector, it is up to individual universities to establish their fees for student attendance. These relatively minimal costs to students in public universities may yet change as the right-wing politicians in Spain, and indeed Greece, influenced by pressure from Europe, push towards implementing big N neoliberal reform of the higher education sector (Hermann 2013, 2015) and change the costs to attend public universities into alignment with private universities. Reputational differences between the public and private sector, where the less expensive public sector boasts the most prestigious institutions, are unlikely to be a significant factor for students in their race to achieve graduate status. Institutional reputation is arguably less of a concern than gaining a degree, given the demand for graduate status by the majority of employers in Spain, Greece and indeed the United Kingdom.

YOUTH UN/EMPLOYMENT IN ENGLAND

But what about the situation facing those young people who have decided to pursue non-graduate employment, rather than academic further and higher education in England? What does the landscape look like for this group? As Brown et al. (2011: 114) point out 'unemployment has risen and wages have fallen around the world'. England has not been immune to this trend: a quick glance at the popular press reveals a disparaging story of shrinking employment opportunities for young people, particularly those without formal further and higher education qualifications. The ONS (2010 in Boffey 2015) figures have shown that in the United Kingdom in 2010 'the number of 16- to 24-year-olds out of work increased by 28,000 to 943,000, one of the highest figures since records began in 1992, giving a youth jobless rate of 19.8%'. More recently, according to Boffey (2015):

> Young people are nearly three times more likely to be unemployed than the rest of the population, the largest gap in more than 20 years, according to an analysis of official figures.

The unemployment rate in England in 2015 was 5.7%, but according to the ONS (2015 in O'Neill 2016) the unemployment figures for the 16–24 youth age group increased to 14.4%. In the year from February 2015 to February 2016 the House of Commons briefing paper on Youth Unemployment Statistics claims that the number of unemployed young people is reducing so that the current 'unemployment rate (the proportion of the economically active population who are unemployed) for 16-24 year olds was 13.6%' (O'Neill 2016: 2). The decrease in the numbers of young people unemployed has been impacted by the government's move to make some form of education (i.e. academic or vocational) compulsory for young people until the age of 18 (Brown et al. 2011), a strategy deployed by many governments in the global north to reduce youth unemployment. A further factor in the reduction to youth unemployment has been the proliferation of zero hours contracts where employers determine the hours an employee works, which can be anything from zero to full time, but the employer has no obligation to provide a minimum number of hours to be worked.

For young people without graduate status the possibilities to secure anything beyond casualised, unskilled employment is increasingly unlikely. According to Ainley and Allen (2010: 4), even if the economy begins to recover:

> There will be a ratchet effect which will raise the bar to worthwhile employ-ment at the same time as qualification inflation continues to devalue all qualifications with the effect that participating in education is like running up a down escalator.

Indeed, the issue of credentialisation of the labour market is a problem that has faced young people from all social and ethnic backgrounds for some time. Blanchflower and Freeman (2000: 19) highlight that throughout the OECD countries, 'young people had greater problems in the job market in the 1990s than in earlier decades'. The problems refer to reduced wages for young people and higher rates of unemploy-ment. These changes have happened despite some favourable economic conditions including the expansion of service industry jobs and greater levels of participation in education, which has reduced the number of youths entering the job market (Blanchflower and Freeman 2000). Indeed, in the United Kingdom, since New Labour was elected to government in 1997, participation in higher education increased by 30%, highlighting the reduction in numbers of young people available to join the employment market (Ainley and Allen 2010). Yet this increase in university participation has since coincided with the 2007 economic crash in the global north and this has restricted the avail-ability of youth employment as young people have to contend with increased competition from older generations seeking work (Ainley and Allen 2010).

There are still opportunities to undertake apprenticeships in a variety of different sectors, although this pathway, which enables young people to 'earn while you learn', is contracting every year (Ainley and Allen 2010). Once a reliable pathway for many of the working classes, and the voca-tionally orientated middle-class young person, the possibilities to secure an apprenticeship 'have all but vanished' (Ainley and Allen 2010: 42). Yet as Cohen points out (2006: 109):

At a time when the job for life has for many, been replaced by the short term contract, the constructs of apprenticeship or career may no longer correspond to any real opportunity structure; yet as a biographical imaginary they may retain salience.

Perhaps this salience is in part responsible for the government's claims that it has rescued apprenticeships 'raising the number available to a quarter of a million, legislating, so that every "suitably qualified" person will have the right to an apprenticeship (HM Government 2009: 58)' (cited in Archer et al. 2010: 126). However, as Archer et al. (2010: 126) note, the term 'suitably qualified' indicates that qualifications are now required to enter a 'route into professions for those without qualifications', revealing a significant shift in the ideology underpinning access to apprenticeships. They have become a somewhat reified pathway, no longer aimed at working-class, disadvantaged young people, but a fall-back option for less academically capable middle-class young people. Thus the former Coalition government and current Conservative government have arguably paid lip service to calls from employers and parents to increase high-quality apprenticeships (Office for Standards in Education, Children's Services and Skills (OFSTED) 2015) and ensure open access to them for all young people, regardless of their social identity and prior academic attainment.

The striking feature of the contemporary youth un/employment market is that of precarity. Bourdieu (1999) described the post-modern context as being influenced by the policy of precarisation. Bauman (2005: 124) defines precarisation as

the ploys that result in the situation of the subjects becoming more insecure and vulnerable and therefore even less predictable and controllable.

Butler (2004, 2008, 2009) distinguishes between 'precariousness', which refers to the corporeal vulnerability shared by all individuals including the privileged, and 'precarity', which, according to Watson (2012), refers to the particular vulnerability experienced by the poor and the disenfranchised. Minimising the impact and influence of precarity, as described by Butler (2009) is reflected in the increasingly individualised and atomised approach taken by young people navigating the youth employment market (Ainley and Allen 2010). The casualisation of non-graduate work, the level of competition for unskilled and semi-skilled service sector work and the significant reduction in all forms of work since 2007 (Brown et al. 2011) has reshaped and restructured the youth employment market to reflect the precarious conditions prevalent in the twenty-first century.

YOUTH UN/EMPLOYMENT IN GREECE AND SPAIN

The final section in this chapter sets out the youth un/employment situation in Greece and Spain to explore the possibilities available to those young people not seeking to pursue an undergraduate programme of study. The context in both Greece and Spain is remarkably similar to that of England; rising rates of youth unemployment proliferate in both countries since the financial crash of 2007. According to Herman (2015):

> Greece suffered from five straight years of economic contraction and lost about a quarter of its GDP. Negative or slow growth is complemented by record-high unemployment, accounting for more than 25% of all workers in Greece and Spain, and for more than 50% of young workers in both countries (for Greece, see Karamessini 2010; for Spain, Banyuls and Recio 2012).

Young people have experienced the sharp end of economic contraction and the resultant strain on their ability to gain secure, long-term employment. Indeed, employers in Greece have extended probation periods to 12 months and Spain has legislated in favour of employers to 'dismiss workers without reason in their first year of employment' (Hermann 2013: 5). Employers in Spain and Greece are more likely to offer short term insecure contracts that on average last for one month.

In terms of Spain, Anxo et al. (2010: 292) draw attention to the proliferation of temporary contracts and note that:

> The high rate of temporary employment has spread from the private sector, where it is more than 30 per cent, to the public sector. In the latter, it has reached 22.8 per cent.

Young people and women have been disproportionately impacted by the increase in temporary employment (Croxford et al. 2006). The gendering of employment opportunities is, in part, informed by the typically hegemonic role of the family in Spain, where women have tended to predominate in family care work and men are overwhelmingly the breadwinners

(Banyuls and Recio 2012). Unqualified young women seeking work rather than higher education are at a double disadvantage in their capacity to secure employment when compared with their male counterparts, evidencing the role of identity in the possibility of accessing employment opportunities.

The employment context in Greece has similarly impacted on young people. Following the financial crash, Greece introduced austerity measures that would see it aim to cut public spending by 18% of Gross Domestic Product (GDP) (Hermann 2013). This dramatic contraction of the public sector has impacted on public and private sector job availability. Leschke et al. (2012) have argued that the unequal impact of the financial crisis on young people is due to the growth in temporary contracts and a social context where temporary workers are the first to lose their jobs. Young people are disproportionately impacted by this insecure employment context as they compete with older, more experienced workers.

To sum up, the financial crisis has reshaped the opportunities available to young people from diverse social backgrounds, but this reshaping has disproportionately impacted on those from disadvantaged backgrounds, with women substantially more affected than their male counterparts due to lingering inequalities originating from the construction of femininity in Spain and Greece (Croxford et al. 2006) that typically requires them to take on caring roles within the family.

Concluding Remarks: The Changing Content of Further Education, Higher Education and the Youth Employment Market

Throughout this chapter I have argued that the further and higher education policy context exerts a defining influence over who can study, what they can study and where they can study. But of course policy changes do not operate in isolation and are a product of the wider social context, which in England, Greece and Spain, has resulted in substantial contractions in the labour market due to ongoing economic austerity. The rising cost of education in England is arguably a barrier to access for disadvantaged young people, largely because of the high levels of personal debt associated with participation in higher education (Wilkins et al. 2013).

The reduction in employment opportunities and apprenticeships for young people has pushed more of them into higher education, perhaps without due consideration of their suitability to, and desire for, higher-level studies. The current education and employment context in the global north is one of insecurity and greater indebtedness. This insecure social context raises social justice questions about which young people can draw on familial and educational resources to ensure their own opportunity is maximised, in a world of shrinking access, opportunities and possibilities.

The widening participation agenda sought to improve access to higher education for non-traditional students. However, research by Medway et al. (2003: 39) noted that staff are encountering students 'whose most salient characteristic, in the teacher's immediate perception, is what they don't know and can't do', and thus non-traditional students are constructed as 'deficit'. Moreover, non-traditional students are frequently blamed for lowering standards and dumbing down higher education syllabuses (Sinfield et al. 2003; Medway et al. 2003). Medway et al. (2003: 39) point out that staff at one London university 'had been noted to say 'our students are thick'' and 'we have great difficulty with our students, they're not what they were'. It seems that 'regulation of desire, not education' is the real aim of current higher education provision (Lillis 2001: 3). At this point it is possible to see that such a deficit model is also bound up in the concept of institutional habitus, where working-class students are on the outside of the institution's habitus (Reay 2001). Thus Medway et al. (2003: 16) argue that:

> HEI's (higher education institutions) need to undergo more deep-seated changes in their 'institutional habitus' that is the nature of the cultural practices, values, priorities and social relationships which characterise the institution.

To improve social justice outcomes, it is not just the student who has to change, but also the higher education institution. Non-traditional students arguably tend to find themselves needed within higher education to meet the governments targets, yet not always wanted, evident via the exclusionary practices of institutional habitus. Therefore, it is possible to see that the absence of 'patterns of association' (Power and Gewirtz 2001: 41) of shared habitus between non-traditional students and their higher education institutions can lead to a situation where they are positioned as outsiders looking in (Sinfield et al. 2003).

To explore these arguments in relation to the experiences of real children from real families, the next chapter explores the case study data, focusing on the post-16 educational plans for the future in the current policy landscape reported by 22 young people.

NOTE

1. In England, older, (pre-1992) universities are more prestigious and selective than newer (post-1992) universities, which were formally called Polytechnics or Colleges of Higher Education, and were granted university status by the Conservative Government in 1992.

Post-16 Educational Choices and Decision-Making: The Role of Policy and Identity

INTRODUCTION

This chapter explores the post-16 educational opportunities available to 22 young people aged 15–16 years located in one outer London Academy School, formerly a comprehensive school until 2012. I will focus on the access and opportunities that the participants perceive are available to them in relation to their post-16 educational pathways. The chapter examines the ways in which recent and radical changes to the further education policy context enable and/or constrain the students in accessing their chosen pathways (Ball et al. 2000). The chapter pays particular attention to the impact of the cuts to the EMA in England, a £30 weekly allowance paid to economically disadvantaged students to support and facilitate their further education studies, typically paid to 16–18-year-olds. The chapter also examines how the participants' gender, social class and ethnicity have influenced their perceptions of their post-16 educational possibilities. The discussion and analysis highlights the complexity of the current educational landscape in terms of the participants' perceptions of the breadth of the choices available to them. The data in this chapter illustrates how recent policy changes in post-16 education provision have influenced the participants' post-16 decisions. I then discuss how aspects of the participants' identity – that is their gender, social class and ethnicity – have influenced their decisions

© The Author(s) 2017
K. Hoskins, *Youth Identities, Education and Employment,*
Policy and Practice in the Classroom,
DOI 10.1057/978-1-137-35292-7_3

about their post-16 pathways. As such, this chapter explores the following questions in relation to post-16 pathways:

1. How have aspects of the participants' gender, social class and ethnicity influenced their decisions about their post-16 pathways?
2. How are the participants' choices and experiences influenced by the impact of cuts to EMA?
3. How are the participants' plans for their post-16 pathways influenced by the current employment context?
4. How does the research cohort decide upon their post-16 and post-18 pathways given the resources and support available to them from their parents and teachers?

The recent changes to further education policies, discussed in Chapter 2, are influencing young people's decisions about their future lives. The range of possible future horizons available to young people post-16 is influenced by the financial resources within their family combined with the external financial resources that they are able to access, which have become increasingly strained since the removal of EMA which would have assisted some students with participation in further education. Policy changes are an important influence on the opportunities as well as the constraints facing young people as they choose the future.

Existing research explores the experiences of young people's education and how their social identity influences choices about further and higher education and employment pathways (Archer et al. 2010; Blanden and Machin 2007; Reay et al. 2005). Other studies have focused on illuminating the choices and transitions undertaken by young people moving on from compulsory education (Derrick et al. 2008; Ecclestone et al. 2009; Ball et al. 2000). Research by Reed et al. (2007) has focused on the suitability and accessibility of post-compulsory education available and has explored the advice available to young people seeking to make the transition into FE. These studies have provided invaluable insights into the intersections between aspects of young people's identities and the interplay of this with their transition choices. However, in the current context, the rapidly changing policy milieu is producing unprecedented transformations to post-16 horizons for action. This has created new and complex choices for the young people I interviewed. In this chapter, I argue that social identity and policy are significant factors that will shape these horizons for action available to young people.

The chapter utilises the theoretical concepts of habitus, field and social capital as set out in Chapter 1 to explore how the participants' social class background has influenced their choice making processes, particularly in relation to the role of family support (Bourdieu 1977). I draw on social constructionist theory to investigate the influence of gender and ethnicity on the participants' subject choices at 16 (Berger and Luckmann 1966; Burr 2003).

THE CHANGING FURTHER EDUCATION POLICY LANDSCAPE: REMOVAL OF EMA

As argued in Chapter 2, the removal of EMA has implications for the possible post-16 transitions available to young people. There were four students in my research sample who would have received the weekly EMA of £30. These four young people felt that it was incredibly unfair that it had been cut, particularly as none of them qualified for the replacement, 16–19-year-old, bursary-funding provision. Georgia, Sian, (both white British, working class), Ann (Black African-Caribbean, working class) and Kim (Chinese, working class) were disappointed about the removal of the EMA funds, which they cited as necessary to enable them to continue with their further education pathways. They reported a cumulative disappointment at being the year group who were hit by further education funding cuts and significant increases in the cost of higher education tuition fees to come if they pursued graduate qualifications. Georgia (white British, working class) told me that 'it is just so annoying, because it's always our year, like they got rid of the EMA when we came'. Sian similarly found the removal of EMA frustrating:

> I think that's so annoying, because if they were still doing the EMA they'd have much better attendance, because loads of people would make more effort to come into school. It's just annoyed me, because my friends that have been a year above me, they don't care about anything, like they still get the EMA, and they don't really do anything, just because they sit in school, and like people that actually work hard, like me, don't even get anything.
> (Sian, white British, working class)

Sian's sense of injustice about the year above receiving EMA because in her view 'they don't care about anything [...] they don't really do anything' highlights some of the wider tensions identified by the government in terms of paying EMA. On the one hand, EMA was credited by UCAS with enabling disadvantaged students greater access to further education (Chowdry et al. 2008); on the other hand, EMA was positioned by the former Coalition Government as too expensive, inefficient and a way of enticing students to participate in further education regardless of their suitability for, and interests in, further studies (McCrone et al. 2010). Heathfield and Fusco (Heathfield and Fusco 2015) have argued that in reality, the removal of EMA has resulted in young people paying the price for austerity, which they had no part in creating, highlighting the inequality and injustice disadvantaged students face in continuing with further education.

The House of Commons Education Committee (2012: 33) noted that 'the loss of EMA would mean that less well-off students might need to take part time jobs' and drew attention to the disadvantage this would put them at, in comparison to their financially better-off peers. Indeed, amongst the students in my study, the most frequently voiced difficulty relating to the removal of EMA was the financial pressure these students were experiencing to make up this lost income. Their families simply could not meet the financial deficit and so inevitably, the removal of EMA resulted in these young people seeking paid employment. As Georgia explained:

> You have to get a part-time job to make up the money...and that means I don't get to go out [...] so then you are focusing on that (paid employment), and then you've got other work to do, it's hard to balance it all. (Georgia, white British, working class)

Not having the funds to socialise may not appear to be an unreasonable price to pay for participation in further education. But Georgia, Sian, Ann and Kim emphasised that they were often tired because of the long hours they spent studying and the relatively long hours they spent working in casualised, semi-skilled employment. The related problem they had all experienced was the difficulty in finding such employment (Blanchflower and Freeman 2000; Evans and Shen 2010). As Georgia noted, 'there's like no jobs now either'. The data indicates that the removal of EMA has contributed to inequality between those who do and those who do not have to work whilst studying and this difference in time pressures will arguably impact on academic outcomes.

According to Sian, the pressure to balance study with her paid employment was a real problem. She told me that:

> I like work as a waitress, but the hours are so bad, but it's because it's the only job I could find, and I was looking for so long, but yesterday I didn't get home until twelve, and I'm working again tonight, and it's just so annoying because I get so tired, but I can't imagine not having the money now, I couldn't stop working. (Sian, white British, working class)

In the current and prolonged economic context of unprecedented government funding cuts in Britain and across the rest of Europe, particularly to further and higher education provision, young people are under increasing pressure to secure further education, whilst simultaneously attempting to hold down semi-skilled or unskilled employment in the unstable, precarious employment market (Ainley and Allen 2010; Archer et al. 2010).

In the interviews, the discussions about EMA contributed to a sense of them and us in the participants' talk about accessing further education between those who do and those who do not qualify for the money. During the focus group with Jen (white British, working/middle class) and Paul (white British, working/middle class), it became clear that they both viewed the removal of EMA as appropriate and fair, as evidenced in the following exchange:

Jen: I don't think EMA's fair in a way, because didn't they get thirty pound a week?

KH: They did, yes.

Jen: I don't get that. I wouldn't be entitled to get that, but I don't get that from my parents or anything [...] and I can't find a job. I wouldn't be able to ask for thirty pound every week, and they just get it...I know it sounds really horrible, when they've got it given to them...

Paul: I think, I don't think...I wouldn't say that for education your costs are thirty pound a week, personally. I wouldn't say that every week I'm going to be spending thirty pound on education, because a pen and a notepad don't cost that much...

KH: Some of it might go on travel maybe, and lunch maybe, that's where the money might go.

Paul: But to be honest you probably need lunch anyway, at home.

This exchange could be interpreted as evidence that these young people are highly individualised in their approach to further education and a typical reflection of a generation described as strategic and self-centred (Beck 1998). However, according to Beck (1998: 36) in post-modern society, 'people are invited to constitute themselves as individuals: to plan, understand and design themselves as individuals'. These students were perhaps individualised in their approach to EMA, but they were simultaneously reflexive, evidenced when Jen defended her views by saying, 'I know what I'm saying sounds really horrible...especially when they've got the money given to them'. They displayed compassion and understanding along with indignation and indifference in almost equal measure.

There were several young people in my sample who were on the margins in financial terms; those who described their family background as middle class, but could be placed, in terms of parental occupation, as lower middle class or upper working class. To refer to the BBC's (BBC Science 2013) detailed and comprehensive seven social class classification schemes, both Jen and Paul are located in families that have represented the bottom four classifications at different moments in time. These four classifications are defined as follows:

New affluent workers – a young class group which is socially and culturally active, with middling levels of economic capital.

Traditional working class – scores low on all forms of capital, but is not completely deprived. Its members have reasonably high house values, explained by this group having the oldest average age at 66.

Emergent service workers – a new, young, urban group which is relatively poor, but has high social and cultural capital.

Precariat, or precarious proletariat – the poorest, most deprived class, scoring low for social and cultural capital.

These newly defined social class boundaries reflect the complex social and economic spaces that these two participants occupied. Jen and Paul's perceptions of who should qualify for EMA were, understandably, subjectively prejudiced by their own narratives and family experiences; both students are from working-class backgrounds and both reported that they had experienced financial hardship. They had also just missed out on qualifying for the funds and felt that this situation was unfair and unjust.

Similarly Claudia (white British), who is from a middle-class background, viewed the funds as too generous and not legitimately required by the majority of students who received them. She told me in the focus group that in her view:

Claudia: Everyone I spoke to had EMA before... they just didn't really, to be honest, apart from my mates who have to spend money to get to school on the train, the school provides textbooks, you are not going to spend thirty pound a week on pencils and pens. That money was being wasted.

KH: So you think it's sort of OK that it's been cut?

Claudia: Yeah. We never had it, so we don't know what we are missing.

Claudia invoked the idea that the students – apart from her friends, who legitimately spent the money – wasted the money and as such, it was appropriate that EMA was discontinued. Her views followed the concerns expressed by McCrone et al. (2010) about the efficiency and fairness of EMA. She was not concerned that her peers in genuine economic need were not going to receive the funds, and she seemed relieved that this unfair funding practice would no longer continue, because in her view those who wanted to participate in further education 'would find the money from somewhere'. Such a view has been contested by The House of Commons Education Committee (2012: 33) who acknowledge that the 'EMA released young people from dependence on their parents, who might not otherwise have provided the financial support necessary' for their further education. The loss of financial autonomy by some young people, albeit in relation to a relatively small amount of income, could effectively price them out of participating in further education, which has potentially serious consequences for social mobility (Hoskins and Barker 2016).

The participants were (almost without exception) aware that their particular year group was losing out in the education game because of recent policy changes, including the removal of EMA. However, the scrapping of EMA had not impacted on the majority of the participants and these young people concurred that their opportunities to access further education would not be influenced by this policy change. To sum up, 18 of the 22 participants felt that scrapping EMA was the right thing for the government to do, but interestingly, none of these students would have qualified to receive it, perhaps reinforcing their individualised views about funding for further education (Giddens 1991). However, four participants viewed the loss of EMA as a real problem for their further education studies and perceived that this had created a financial burden that would negatively impact their academic outcomes.

Removal of EMA: The Teachers' Perspectives

Interestingly, the seven teachers I interviewed had a different perspective on the impact that the removal of EMA was having on their students, particularly in terms of participation. All of the teachers perceived that the removal of EMA was a significant factor in some students' decisions not to return to the school for their A-levels. As Daniel explained:

> I think cutting EMA has made an impact, and I've had a conversation with students who said some of their friends would have come back if the EMA was still available for students. On the other hand, some students may have come back just to get the EMA, and I did wonder the value of some students coming back to school, perhaps not performing in year twelve, and then finding they've got to go and do something else. But I certainly think, if it's targeted correctly, I think for the vast majority of students it was certainly useful. As far as a drop in numbers, I don't know yet if we'll drop in numbers of students. (Daniel, White British, Year 12/Post 16 Teacher)

Daniel had concerns about the legitimacy of all students' claims on EMA, noting that some students would have returned just to receive the money. However, he is also aware that the school's FE participation numbers have been adversely impacted by the removal of these funds. He talked about a small yet significant group of students who were not academically motivated, but wanted to participate in further education to gain some form of vocational qualification and it was this group that was suffering.

Similarly, Julia and Chloe noted that for some students, receiving the EMA funds were genuinely useful and a necessity to enable their participation in further education. Chloe noted that the school's local context and demographic meant that the removal of EMA was less of an issue for Parkfield School. They explained the removal of EMA as follows:

> I've been here for quite a while; I've seen students who didn't have anything, then obviously I saw them get it, then I've seen them lose it. There is no doubt that for a handful of students it does make a difference to have it,

obviously it makes their life easier. (Julia, White Irish, Year 12/Post 16 Teacher)

In terms of EMA I think it's made it tougher for some kids, definitely, in terms of...especially commuting to college or sixth form, and bits like that, but in terms of books we do provide books and things like that, resources, so they haven't missed out on resources in the same way that other students might, who go to tertiary sixth form colleges will. I don't think it's dissuaded that many students from coming to sixth form at the moment, but it's possibly something we'll be seeing in the longer run, when the kind of stats are in...I think it's a shame, I think it's something that does help our students, some of our students who want to stay on, stay on. As I say that is a minority group here. (Chloe, White British, Year 12/Post 16 Teacher)

Chloe was aware of the negative impact the removal of EMA had on some students, but acknowledged that this is a minority group within the school. Whereas Jasper took a slightly different view to the question about the removal of EMA. He perceived the impact on the students to be of greater significance than Chloe. He explained that:

To the school I don't see any sort of impact, for students I do believe it has an impact, in so much that it may stop some students carrying on to the sixth form. We've not seen a real decrease in numbers but obviously it's a perceptual thing. I believe that the students believe they can't afford to carry on, so this alternative of not studying, of going to work and earning money, always seems more attractive. So in my lessons we talk about it occasionally. It doesn't come up in my content, what I teach, but comes up in just general chit chat...and if I compare, I've been here eight, nine years, financial concerns are a lot more than they were back then. Students are more aware of the financial impact, and the financial impact is now, I believe for some students, not all but some, is driving their decisions whether to stay in education or to go out and get a job. (Jasper, White British, Year 12/Post 16 Teacher)

Jasper points to the tension produced for some disadvantaged students who do not have the funds to continue in further education without the money provided by EMA. Indeed, the House of Commons Education Committee (2012: 33) noted that the EMA 'enabled low income families to see further education as an option for them' and that for some families 'the lack of guaranteed funding as a "safety net" would deter some young people from applying for courses', highlighting the disadvantage that would face some young people when these funds were removed. Emily noted the potential negative impact on some students, particularly the pressure to replace the EMA money through paid employment, which she perceived would impact on their time to study. She told me that:

> Obviously I think it is going to have an impact on students, because obviously it's going to impact whether they go to university, whether they stay on at the school, you know. Money, money in the sense of are they going to have enough money for books, resources, what they want to do? So I think, you know, you do have students who work in the evenings, you are going to have an impact on the homework, students working at weekends, students working up through the mocks, so it's not an equal playing field, you know, they are trying to compete with students who are in private school with smaller classes, they are competing with people here who don't have to work, and I think the hours that students actually work, I don't think the government are quite aware of, and also the four AS levels they are juggling. You know, the time requirements are intense. (Emily, Head of Post 16 Study Sociology, white British)

Emily was aware of the tension facing her students in terms of the money that they needed to make up to be able to fund their further education. A National Union of Teachers (NUT) (2012: 12) survey exploring teachers' views on changes to 14–19 education revealed a general level of concern about the removal of EMA amongst teachers and that 'overall the responses suggest that the removal of EMA has been damaging'. Part of the EMA removal problem highlighted by teachers in the NUT survey related to the increased risk of some disadvantaged young people falling into the NEET (Not in Education, Employment or Training) category (Avis 2014). A further and related concern was the pressure to earn money, as Emily had identified. The lack of financial support for disadvantaged young people seeking to pursue further education, coupled with the competition for semi-skilled or service sector work could result in many younger people finding themselves categorised as a NEET.

John's concerns also highlighted the financial pressure created by the removal of EMA, noting that the distraction of paid work could impact negatively on schoolwork. But he also commented on the widening gap between advantaged, middle-class young people and disadvantaged, working-class young people. He made a distinction between those who do and those who do not have additional resources to draw upon. He explained that:

> I think for those that didn't get the money, I don't know if it's actually stopped some of them coming into sixth form or carrying on. I think if anything it would have just pushed them, either they've got to go and get a job, get work, which again, you know, because they do a lot of work in school, means they are more distracted from doing schoolwork. And I would say it probably doesn't help with that gulf does it, between students, because some are getting help and some are not [...]. Particularly when you are maybe in a school that does have quite a lot of students who are maybe from higher income backgrounds, because it's making that gap a bit wider again. (John, Head of Post 16 Study, white British)

The issue of the growing gap between advantaged and disadvantaged groups has long been a concern in terms of educational access and outcomes (see, e.g., Croll 2004; Devine 2004; Lareau 2004; Power et al. 2003; Reay 2006; Reay et al. 2013). The removal of EMA is part of a wider, neo-liberal policy agenda that has resulted in the gradual withdrawal of the state from many areas and levels of educational provision. The shifts that have taken place have negatively impacted on the gap between rich and poor students in schools in England, emphasising the inequality experienced by some and highlighting the abundance of resources possessed by others.

Finally, Maria reflected on the replacement scheme that had been introduced by the government, noting that the scope seems to be greatly reduced to that of EMA:

> I do think that, they have brought out what they call an equivalent, which is the bursary, and schools do have access to a bursary programme, for students of low income, but from what I know it's not as far reaching as EMA was. I think it has had a knock-on effect, you know, a lot of students, you hear anecdotally in class, quite a few students saying they are going to miss their EMA. A couple of students, when it came to retaking their exams, we had one student last year, and she didn't want to retake her exams, because she couldn't afford the retake fee because her family were low income. Now that's obviously educationally harming her, whereas if she had her EMA she would have been able to pay for the retake. (Maria, White British Year 12/ Post 16 Teacher)

Maria was aware that students were dissatisfied about the removal of EMA and that they would miss the funds. The example of a student unable to pay for a retake examination reveals the potentially damaging impact of not providing funds to disadvantaged students. The example also reinforces the negative impact on social mobility for those students from low-income families who simply cannot cover the costs of their child's education themselves (Barker and Hoskins 2015).

The teachers I interviewed were all aware that removing EMA had negatively impacted on some of their students' chances of staying on in school. The student and teacher voices highlight the concerns raised by the House of Commons Education Committee (2012) who have vociferously criticised the government for the hasty policy u-turn they performed when they went back on their pre-election pledge and removed EMA. The young people interviewed in my study belong to an arguably disadvantaged generation, and this is particularly apparent in relation to the further and higher education possibilities available to them and also their employment potential. Jones (2014: 96) argues that young people today are facing an increasingly precarious social context:

> Britain is edging towards a common European condition, in which younger workers experience not only unemployment but a wider precariousness that includes issues of pay, job security, housing – most of the resources that are needed for an independent life. At the same time educational provision is being reduced and rationed.

The removal of EMA has certainly reduced academic and vocational educational opportunities for the most disadvantaged young people to pursue FE, thus inhibiting the potential for young people to achieve intra-generational social mobility. Somewhat ironically, the current government, which was instrumental in the decision to remove EMA, claims that improving intra-generational social mobility is a key goal for their current term in office (Social Mobility and Child Poverty Commission 2015). The removal of EMA revealed that social class background has influenced the participants' choices in a range of different ways. To understand the role of identity in the participants' choices, the chapter now explores the role of gender in shaping post-16 choices.

GENDER AND POST-16 SUBJECT CHOICE: 'STATS IS THE GIRLIE VERSION OF MATHS'

The chapter now explores how identity influences post-16 decision-making. In Chapter 1, I argued that aspects of identity including social class, gender and ethnicity have been shown to have a significant influence on education and employment choices and outcomes for young people in a range of national contexts (see, e.g., Ainley and Allen 2010; Archer et al. 2010; Reay et al. 2005; Ball et al. 2000). These studies have highlighted the enduring capacity of identity to act as a predictor of the likely educational and subsequent employment participation for young people. Despite interruptions to this pattern of social reproduction (see, e.g., Reay et al. 2005), it remains the case that family background, cultural orientation and gender alongside geographical context are important components in shaping the likelihood of successful academic outcomes (Hoskins and Ille 2016). In England, identity and social context act as powerful influences with the capacity to shape the life trajectory of individuals. These influences linger despite state intervention through policy initiatives in many areas of people's lives, including social welfare, health care and education, to address some of the structural inequality that persists. Discourses of equality and achievement for all, which are maintained and circulated by the state (see, e.g., DfE, Department for Education 2011), are hard to fulfil in an unequal society that values different identities in different ways (Wilkinson and Pickett 2010).

The empirical data I gathered reveal some of the advantages possessed by those students with a more 'successful' academic identity, that is, those who are from a privileged family background, those who understand the demands associated with achieving examination success and those who are hardworking and ambitious for their future. In the following sections I explore how the participants' identities have influenced their post-16 subject choices to understand if and how gender, social class and/or ethnicity shapes their educational decisions.

The most apparent aspect of identity impacting on the participants' post-16 subject choices was their gender. Focus group one was the only group not to comment on the impact of their gender on their post-16 and post-18 choices. For participants in focus groups two, three, four and five, gender was a salient influence, shaping their aspirations and expectations for the future. But interestingly, when I asked the students if they felt that their gender had influenced their post-16 educational choices many of them strongly rejected this suggestion. For example, in focus group two, Holly (white British, unsure of class background/probably middle class), Claire (white Irish, working class), Susie (white British, middle class), Julie (white British, middle class) and Jamal (Pakistani, unsure of class background) told me that gender had not influenced their subject choices in any way and that they were free to choose whatever they wanted. Yet further probing revealed a gendered story:

> *KH*:   Do you think your gender has influenced your choices?
> *Holly*:   Not very much really... Like the subjects I do are quite mixed, like there are not really boys and girls in any particular subject.
> *Claire*: What about Sociology!
> *Holly*:   Ok yeah, apart from sociology. Apart from that there's a real mix. So it doesn't really matter, like there's no gender differentiation kind of thing.
> *Susie*:   I do English literature, sociology obviously, history and classics. So there's quite, there is a mix there, and my subjects are the kind of things that boys and girls are both interested in, there's no stigma... Like if a boy wants to do sociology, like Jamal, nobody's gonna take the mick or hold it against him.
> *Claire*: Boys even do textiles... But there are no boys in my textiles class, but a few years ago there was a boy who did textiles.
> *KH*   There was one? (GROUP LAUGHTER)
> *Julie*:   I do textiles, ICT and business, and sociology, but like ICT and business are sort of mixed, because I think that's something everyone can have, but then textiles it's all girls, and sociology is mainly girls, a few boys. But I don't know, I don't think it really matters, if a boy wanted to do textiles I don't think it would be... you know... He wouldn't not do it because of the girls. I think everyone sort of knows what they want to do and they'll just do it.
> *Jamal*:   I agree with what Julie said, but like I think from since I've been young I've kind of been socialised into what a boy would do, for example I don't really like essay writing and stuff like that. The reason I picked sociology, in the beginning, to be honest, it was just the last subject in the blocks.

The subtle gendering shaping the students' decisions about subject choices is apparent here, despite their claims that boys and girls are not constrained by their gender when it comes to subject choice. Jamal made reference to his socialisation as a boy and acknowledged that this had played some part in his choice making processes. Riddell's (2012) study exploring gender and the politics of school subject choice similarly found that young people could not easily identify how gender had shaped their choices and experiences and yet it had been a factor. The exchange does reveal that the girls in focus group four were undertaking a range of different subjects, some of which are more strongly socially constructed as being masculine subjects, such as ICT and business studies, suggesting there has been movement towards more gender balanced choices (Francis 2000; Kenway et al. 1998). However, Francis (2006: 58) also notes that 'as soon as choice is reintroduced at post-16, gender re-emerges as a factor in subject uptake'. Thus the gendering of the students' subject choices was apparent in relation to focus group two.

In focus group four, there was a similarly strong sense for Claudia (white British, middle class), Kim (Chinese, working class) and Adrian (white British, middle class) that gender had not impacted on their post-16 subject choices. The discussion of post-16 choices overlapped with their decisions about university courses, as evidenced in the following exchanges:

KH: So do you think your choices are influenced by your gender?
Claudia: I don't know, I don't think my gender really affects what I want
         to do...
KH   What do you study?
Claudia: Psychology. I guess that's kind of...more girls would do
         psychology than guys maybe, but I find it the most interest-
         ing subject so I want to go and do it. I don't really think my
         gender affects...it really, it's just something that I want to
         study. I don't think gender really comes into it, to be honest.
         I think nowadays there's such a big emphasis on equality that
         it's [gender inequality] almost been eradicated from the whole
         system. I don't think there's any preferential treatment...So
         I don't think me being a girl influenced my choices at all,
         because anthropology [preferred university subject choice],
         I believe there's quite an even mix of men and women in
         there, and I think it's a subject that focuses on looking at
         people as a whole, not dividing into different groups. So
         I don't think I was, I wasn't really influenced by being a girl.
Kim: I'm doing English, which I think is quite generic. I don't know,
         I think everyone has their preferences, there are always these
         stereotypes that boys like sciences and girls like English, but

from going to open days and stuff I think the amount of boys and girls was quite even, who was in the room. It seemed equal.

Adrian: Well I'm doing maths now and there's like two girls in my class. Lots of boys take it, but there's nothing to say if you are a girl and you want to take it then you can't, it's no difference.

Kim: I'm doing stats…But stats is sort of like a girlie version of maths! Our class is mostly girls!

Adrian: I'm doing mechanics and stats, but if you go into mechanics class there will be a far higher percentage of boys because obviously a lot of the boys want to become engineers, so they take maths. But that's just what people choose to do.

The gendered subject choices are apparent in this exchange. The students' discussions about their subject choices reveal the unproblematic way they understand the influence of their gender on their aspirations and plans for the future. Kim's reference to stats being the 'girlie version of maths' was met with quiet and knowing giggles. Adrian's acknowledgement that his mathematics class is full of boys, because obviously they just 'want to become engineers' highlights a common sense social construction of gender where people just choose a pathway because it is obvious and natural to them (Burr 2003). Although the 'obvious' here relates to the student's gender, the students resisted any such labelling and identified themselves as 'lone agents whose fate depended on their own efforts' (Hoskins and Barker 2014: 14). The literature highlights that subject choice 'has implications for career choices and more recently there has been a marked shift in girls' aspirations' (Francis et al. 2012: 72), with girls aspiring to a wide range of professional occupations. However, the data gathered for this study suggests that more work could usefully be done with young people to reduce the post-16 subject choice gender differences that persist.

In focus group five, Jen and Paul, both white British and from working-class backgrounds, similarly denied that gender had shaped their post-16 subject choices in any way. The following exchange exemplifies their position:

KH: So do you think your gender has influenced your choices?

Jen: Um…I don't think gender's like a huge issue here, because like sociology, I do sociology, and it's sort of mixed, more or less half and half boys and girls, so yeah, I don't…

Paul: I'd say it hasn't affected my choices, but in the subjects I do I do think they are mainly male ... In my maths and further maths class, out of twenty-five students we've got two females, and in economics we've got two females, there's only like four girls in the year doing economics out of about sixty or something. [...] But gender hasn't affected my decision to pick these subjects, but it's just how I've seen it is in the subjects.

Paul's discussion of his subject choices reveals a gendered story. He has selected the typically masculine subjects of mathematics and economics (Francis 2000). Mendick's (2005) research found that of 43 participants in her study, only 4 identified as being good at mathematics and these students were all male. Thus, mathematics is, according to Mendick (2005: 235), 'something that is discursively inscribed as masculine', a finding that resonated with the subject choices made by participants in my study. As Walkerdine (1998) points out, the claims that in the United Kingdom girls and women perform significantly less well than boys and men do on mathematical tasks, activities and examinations can be seen as a social and cultural construction. Walkerdine (1998: 8) argues that in the United Kingdom, 'the powers of rationality and mathematical thinking are so bound up with the cultural definition of masculinity ... that femininity is equated to poor performance even when the girl or woman is perform-ing well'. The socially constructed cultural gender differences between boys and girls have far reaching implications and can negatively distort girls' perceived lack of competency in mathematics. Thus, applying the lens of social constructionism is a way to theorise gendered differences and avoid generalisations about masculine and feminine subjects.

However, there was difference and divergence about the students' perceptions of the influence of gender on their post-16 subject choices. In contrast with focus group two, four and five, Jodie (white British, working class), Sandra (white British, middle class), Adele (Black African-Caribbean, middle class) and Laura (white British, middle class) in focus group three acknowledged that their subject choices were gen-dered in some ways. This is reflected in the following exchange:

KH: In what ways, if any, do you think your post-16 subject choices have been influenced by your gender?

Jodie: A lot ... Because as females we are pressurised to do so much, like we are always going to be compared to the male figure in everything, and because society changes more and more females want to get careers and get their own life, they don't want to be dependent on a man, or their family.

KH: Yes of course. What do you think?

Sandra: Well, because teaching is a very female sort of job, there are loads of females, like in primary school all of my teachers were female, and as I want to move on and teach I think that might have influenced me.

Adele: Yeah, I think as well, because quite a lot of teachers are female, so you sort of look up to them.

KH: OK, but you are doing medicine?

Adele: Yeah, because nursing is more a female job, and doctors are more males… I want to be a doctor. I'm not sure how my gender has influenced that. None of my parents are in the healthcare profession, so I'm not sure…

Laura: I suppose maybe gender has influenced me in a way because I've chosen a subject that is typical for a girl, but there are lots of successful men in the fashion business as well. But when I chose my GCSEs I did graphic design and there was like 25 of us in the class and only four girls, the rest were boys. In my textile class it's all girls. It shows how there is like a clear divide in subjects through gender, but I think also it has like influenced me as well, because I don't want to like, I want to be like an independent woman who has her own money, I don't want to rely on a man.

These responses capture the complexity of subject choice and highlight the myriad ways in which these young women experience and construct their gendered identity. Jodie points out the pressure to 'do everything' and points to the constant comparisons between female and males, where the expectation is that women will become independent, an aspiration noted in Fuller et al.'s (2011) study exploring girls' ambitions for the future. Laura noted the clear gender divide in her subject choices of textiles and graphic design, where one subject is clearly feminised and the other masculinised. This gendering of subjects has made Jodie and Adele more determined to avoid any reliance on a man and instead become independent adults with their own financial security (Fuller et al. 2011).

Laura (white British, middle class) has aspirations to become a teacher in the future, a desire that she attributes to her feminised primary school experiences. The feminisation of education is a widely discussed discourse (Skelton 2002) and feminised schools have somewhat unfairly long been

blamed for failing boys (Epstein et al. 1998) and favouring female pedagogy and assessment patterns (Elwood 2016). Laura is reflexive about the
influence of her primary schooling on her aspirations to become a teacher
and acknowledges that becoming a teacher is a good job for a girl. As
Maguire (1997: 94) notes 'girls and women have traditionally been (re)
produced through discourses of femininity, maternity and caring'. As a
consequence, 'teaching and nursing have long been constructed as "common-sense fillers" between leaving school and starting a family' (Maguire
1997: 94). This common sense, gendered discourse appears to have
influenced Laura's post-16 and subsequent career choices and to have
created a context in which that decision appears to be a natural and easy
choice.

Adele (Black African-Caribbean, middle class) told me that her subject
choices are orientated around her desire to become a doctor. She told me
that she was aware that women tend to choose nursing, but she was not
choosing this pathway. She could not immediately account for her
choices, as her family members are not in the medical profession and are
clustered in white-collar occupations. However, after some reflection, she
told me later in the focus group that her mother had instilled in her a
desire and drive to be successful in her career:

> Since I was younger my mum's always said work as hard as you can, achieve
> your potential, and she is relatively high up in what she does [white collar
> office worker], so that can have an influence...Women now are in the
> higher jobs.

Thus her mother's encouragement was identified as important to Adele's
aspirations for the future. As Jackson and Marsden (1962: 97) found in
their older yet still relevant research, in terms of the significant familial
influences in their sample 'the centre of [educational decision making]
power usually lay with the mother'. However, Jackson and Marsden
(1962: 97) noted that this 'could not be altogether accounted for by the
mother's education or her superior station before marriage, though both
these mattered'. The influence of her mother's guidance was evident in
Adele's future ambitions and she was keen to become a successful doctor
and an independent woman in her adult life.

The data and analysis presented here highlight the continuing influence
of gender on post-16 subject choices and also the participants' future
professional selves. Despite their initial questioning and rejection that

gender could have shaped their choices, as the focus groups progressed it became evident that gender is a salient factor shaping many of my participants' work related ambitions for the future.

Social Class and Post-16 Subject Choice: 'There's a Lot of Council Estates Around Here, but Last Year, There Were Girls Who Had Mini Coopers with Private Number Plates'

I now turn to discuss the potential impact of social class background on the participants' post-16 subject choices. Similarly to gender, social class was not generally perceived as a barrier or a factor in the participants' subject choices. The school is located in a relatively privileged locale, as discussed in Chapter 1, but despite this there are pockets of under-privilege and there were stories of hardships shared in the focus group discussion.

The discussion in focus group one highlighted the students' reluctance to acknowledge any impact of their social class background on their post-16 plans. This reluctance is reflected in the following exchange between Georgia (white British, working class) and Sian (white British, working class):

Georgia: I don't really think it makes a difference, because my mum and dad didn't go to uni and like they don't have really good jobs or anything, but it hasn't put me in like, I haven't thought oh I don't want to, I just want to get an easy job, and at the same time I haven't thought I really want to go to uni and do a lot better, it hasn't really influenced me ... I just feel that I can just, I don't know, it hasn't really pushed me one way or the other, I still just want to do what I want to do, and not really worry about things.

Sian: I think that like seeing how my mum and dad live, and it would be nice if we lived in a big mansion, it sort of pushes you to do well, so you can get the highest jobs and get more money ... Neither of my parents went to uni, but we all know ... if you go to uni it's like known that you can get a better job.

Sian and Georgia, who are both from a working-class background, were eager to resist any social class labelling or generalisations. Neither student had a parent who had participated in higher education, which might have been a factor in their reluctance to discuss any impact of class on their future plans. Sian was aware of the potential gains of attending university in terms of employment prospects. Similar to Skegg's (1997: 57) participants, Sian and Georgia are perhaps constrained by their 'historical legacies', and 'their lack of forms of capital means their access to certain routes such as higher education [...] is already restricted'. As Hodkinson et al. (1996) have noted, processes of socialisation and identity formation help explain why less privileged students remove themselves from higher status choices and trajectories, whilst working to maintain agency in relation to their choices. Georgia in particular could not envisage a future that required her to participate in higher education, but constructed this choice as personal agency.

Paresh (Indian, middle class), also in focus group one, had a different view about the potential impact of social class on her future plans:

Paresh: Well I think it's more based on who you know, rather than your class, because if you know people that work higher up and get you jobs, or get you into there, then obviously you are going to go further.

KH: Do you think who you know is helped by social class?

Paresh: Yeah I really do think it makes a difference.

Paresh, who described herself as from a middle-class Indian background, is aware of the possible advantages conferred by 'who you know' and her narrative alludes, indirectly, to the importance of social capital for accessing social goods. According to Putnam (2001: 171) 'social capital is about networks' first and foremost. The quality of the networks available can have a significant impact on what is and what is not possible, for example, in terms of future employment.

The discussion about the potential impact of social class background on post-16 choices in focus group two reflected a range of different experiences and perceptions, but these were similarly rooted in the participants' perceptions that it was not a significant influence. This is highlighted in the following exchange:

Jamal: I don't think it's had an effect on me to be honest, because the way it would probably be perceived is like middle class or upper class would go to university, and lower class wouldn't, and I'm from a working-class background, so I don't think it's really affected me that much.

Claire: My family's got a working-class background as well, but they've
            always said it doesn't have to stop you, being from where you are
            from, you can do anything kind of thing, and it doesn't really
            matter what class you are part of now, there's less like stigma
            attached to being working class. There's as many opportunities
            there for people from that sort of background as there are for
            people from a middle-class background, it's just easier for middle
            classes because they have more access.

Holly: I don't know, it's quite confusing because my mum's family are
            quite middle class, my dad's family are very working class... But I
            don't believe in working class and middle class... It hasn't
            impacted on my choices.

KH: How about you and social class?

Julie: I think I'm kind of middle class, because my dad has quite a
            middle class job, although he didn't go to uni when he left school.
            My mum's a teacher and she went to uni, but I don't think
            because she went to uni it has any kind of influence on me, I
            don't think it has any effect on my decision.

The discussion here reflects the range of positions taken up by Jamal
(Pakistani, unsure of class background), Claire (white British, working
class), Holly (white British, unsure of class background/probably middle class) and Julie (white British, middle class), and also illustrates
their perception that social class background does not impact on their
post-16 choices and decisions. They display an individualistic perspective towards their identity that does not engage with differences rooted
in social class position. These perceptions are at odds with the research
literature exploring the influence of social class on post-16 pathways.
Bathmaker et al. (2013) argue that working-class students seem to be
disadvantaged, compared with their middle-class peers, by their limited
pre-disposition towards the 'accumulation of additional capitals' and by
limited access to material resources. Yet the participants from working-
class backgrounds in my study resist being positioned as disadvantaged
in relation to their middle-class peers. Despite evidence showing that
social inequalities cannot be overcome by individual reflexivity (Li
2013) and academic aspirations (Reay 2005), many of the young
people in my study seem entrenched within an individualist
perspective.

Discussions in focus group three similarly centred on a reluctance to
acknowledge the influence of social class background on post-16 subject

choices. Jodie (white British, working class) and Laura (white British, middle class) explained that:

Jodie: I'm not sure... I'm probably a mixed social class, because my mum's a teacher, but my dad, he's like a welder, he's quite low down, so my dad's family are very kind of working class, and my mum's family are higher class, so I'm sort of a mix... but I don't think it's influenced my subject choices... I really don't see myself in any way, I just see myself as a person.

Laura: Yeah, I think I agree, you know, it's not something that's labeled, it's what I want to do, what I want to study, it doesn't matter what anyone else is doing.

Jodie and Laura both hoped to become teachers in the future. Laura wanted to become a textiles teacher and Jodie wanted to follow her mum and become a primary school teacher. Jodie described her social class as mixed and later in the focus groups, as more working class than middle class. Laura described herself as from a middle-class family, which she described as 'comfortable'. The different class backgrounds of these two participants and their different family habitus has nevertheless resulted in both students' aspirations for teaching careers. These two respondents seem to confirm McNay's (1996: 1) point that the habitus 'is a generative rather than a determining structure which establishes a creative relation between the subject and the world'. The students' dispositions and inclinations are similar, suggesting that their gender might be a more significant influence than their social-class background in terms of their desire to teach.

However, Adele (Black African-Caribbean, middle class), also from focus group three, did acknowledge that she had friends she had seen influenced by their social class background. She explained that:

Um... I don't think it's affected me personally, but I've seen some of my friends from like south London, it affects them, because they are from like a lower, working class, it's harder for them to get the resources we have, so they end up giving up in education, because they feel they'll always be that class, but I think sometimes it is like, yeah, it affects certain people.

Adele's example of friends who are impacted by their social class also indicates evidence of the impact of intersectional elements of identity –

Adele is African-Caribbean and so are the friends referred to here. Adele's story suggests that her friends might have felt themselves to be 'othered' by an education system that cannot fully engage with cultural and classed differences (Ladson-Billings 2006). Adele also notes that the lack of resources available to her friends to stay in education, highlighting the material impact of poverty. The impact of fewer resources is well documented in the literature, perhaps most notably is the example of research on 9,500 7-year-olds from the Millennium Cohort Study which shows that however good or effective the parents, they cannot overcome the structural problems of poverty (Hartas 2012).

Discussions about social class were minimal in focus group four. Four of the five students are from middle-class, economically privileged backgrounds (based on their descriptions of their parents' occupations). The only working-class student in the group is Kim (Chinese, working class) and she offered the following observation about social class in the school:

> Uh, I don't think it affects, I suppose when everyone comes into this school, from the moment you step in everyone has the same opportunity and treatment... You don't have a higher chance of getting a certain grade for being a different class or whatever, but, you know, I think it's definitely different for university. Big families with financial problems, they'll be more apprehensive about going to university, because especially when there's talk of the degree being devalued, it being a waste of money and you could go straight into work. So I think they'll be more reluctant, because it's a lot of money.

Kim rejects any possible post-16 impact on subject choices arising from social class background on the basis that the school values and ensures equality of opportunity for all pupils. The rest of the group agreed with Kim's sentiment that 'there's no problem here' (Gaine 1995) in terms of social class inequality.

Focus group five participants similarly perceived that social class was not an issue in the school and had not impacted on their subject choices:

> Jen: I don't know, I don't really think there's an issue on social class and what you choose to do, because there's no sort of like image, I don't think here, that says like a lower social class does this subject. I don't think it's affected the subjects I've chosen to do or anything like that.

Paul: I would say the same sort of thing, it's not really down to social class, but choosing subjects or there's not, there's not more different, there's not more of a certain social class in certain subjects, I wouldn't say.

Paul (white British, working class) and Jen (white British, working class) reject the notion that there could be any difference in the social class composition of their subjects, despite some apparently obvious gendered and classed choices; Jen wants to attend university and become a teacher. Paul is studying maths, further maths and economics, which are not typical choices for a working-class boy (Riddell 2012). Perhaps similarly to the academically successful working-class students in Jackson and Marsden (1962) study, these students' academic capability and success has played a part in their rejection of social class as an 'excuse' for not achieving.

The data reveal that the students did not acknowledge the impact of their social class background on their choices. They all emphasised their own agency and tended to embrace an individualist perspective in relation to their education choices. They are not aware that their choices and plans for the future are shaped by the transmission of family resources and dispositions, and by the opportunities of their own time and place. Rather, they construct themselves as reflexive agents of individualism whose decisions are 'pragmatically rational' (Hodkinson et al. 1996; cited in Hoskins and Barker 2014). Their dispositions are overwhelmingly aligned with the formal demands and expectations of the school system. The choices made by students from middle-class families display evidence of social reproduction rather than social mobility so participants with professional parents were influenced by the academic upbringing they had experienced in their childhoods. However, those students whose parents engaged in vocational careers such as plumbers, builders and hairdressers indicated that they aspire to higher status occupations, which is reflected in their post-16 subject choices. These aspirations for higher status employment highlight Parkfield School's success in providing an environment where students from working-class families can strive for social mobility.

The data also revealed the difficulty that many participants had in terms of placing themselves in social class categories. Most of them rejected the idea that social class was a useful or relevant description that applied to their circumstances. The parental occupations reported by the participants revealed myriad new and more traditional forms of work that are undertaken, making social class classifications more complicated for the students.

ETHNICITY AND POST-16 SUBJECT CHOICES

There were far fewer discussions about the influence of ethnicity on post-16 subject choices. However, there were examples where ethnicity was evoked as a significant influence that shaped the participants' subject choices. The range of positions taken up is evident in the following data extracts.

In focus group one, only Paresh (Indian, middle class) is from a minority ethnic background, but she, along with Georgia (white British, working class), Gemma (white British, middle class) and Steph (white British, middle class), resisted the suggestion that ethnicity makes any difference to subject choices at 16:

> *Georgia*:   I don't really think it makes a difference, I've never really had an issue with anything due to it, it's never changed my, I never thought I should do something because I'm white, or anything like that.
> *KH*:   Right, OK.
> *Gemma*:   I don't think it's got much effect on anything.
> *KH*:   Any post-16 subject choices or..?
> *Steph*:   I don't think it makes a difference.
> *KH*:   OK, and how about for you?
> *Paresh*:   Me neither. I know some Asian people, they all do A-levels and then go to uni, and get like, their parents are going to uni and like their parents really drill it into them, but my parents are not really like that.

Georgia's point that her whiteness has not impacted on her decisions and choices resonates with research conducted by Tochluk (2010), who found that whiteness provides more opportunities, particularly in relation to education. Tochluk (2010: 121) reflecting back on her childhood claims that 'we were raised to expect that doors would open for us as long as we put in enough effort' and this reinforced a sense of 'white entitlement'. Perhaps the respondents in focus group one are similarly privileged in relation to their ethnic identity. Paresh also noted that her parents were not like stereotypical Indians in their aspirations for her future and gave her the space to find her own preferences. However, it is possible that Paresh also felt constrained to make a stronger point when surrounded by her white peers.

The discussion in focus group two revealed a more mixed picture with both acknowledgement and resistance that ethnicity had shaped their subject choices:

Claire: I don't really see the difference, like with school, because it's quite different, different ethnicities and stuff, I don't really see anyone like, I don't know how to say it, I don't see the differences in like the opportunities people are going in, like the subjects they choose and the paths they are taking, I don't see differences with like their ethnicity and stuff.

Holly: I don't think for me it's had any impact. I think it just really like, because everyone has the opportunity, they can get loans, it's not like they can't go, it's whether they want to go more. I don't think there's anything stopping people going because they can.

Susie: There's no real, it hasn't affected me at all, like there's obviously . . . the opportunities are there for everyone, there's no discrimination between ethnic groups, like everyone's got the same opportunities, the same rights, the same status in society now, so I don't really see it as a problem, like everyone's equal sort of thing, so, you know, if they want to go to university they can, they've got the means, they've got the opportunities. If they want to go it's their choice.

KH: So it's up to the individual, there's no barriers there?

Julie: It hasn't affected me. I don't think it would affect anyone . . . The only problem would be like secondary schools.

KH: What do you mean?

Julie: The whole labelling, like black boys, their teachers will put them down, and then they might think well, if it's like this here imagine what it's going to be like at uni, much more like professional in a way, much different, it might be daunting and they might not realise that people from all over the world can go to different unis.

Claire (white Irish, working class), Holly (white British, unsure of class background/probably middle class), Susie (white British, middle class) and Julie (white British, middle class) agreed that ethnicity did not impact on their subject choices and was not a factor in their plans for the future. But they raise a number of interesting points, particularly the issue of equality of access to university, which relies heavily on post-16 choices.

The common perception amongst the students is that anyone can access higher education, and ethnicity is not a factor. But these four students are white and perhaps, similar to the participants in focus group one, experience their whiteness as a sense of entitlement (Tochluk 2010). Drawing attention to the widening participation agenda and encouraging academically focused post-16 pathways that could lead to university formed a central strand of Parkfield School's strategy to engage non-traditional students in higher education. The participants in focus group two evoked some of the language used by teachers in the sixth form to encourage engagement and dispel any sense that higher education was anything other than a meritocracy that rewards hard work and achievement.

However, Jamal (Pakistani, unsure of class background) had a different experience. He told me that the school had identified him to attend a programme aimed at increasing access to higher education for Black and Minority Ethnic (BME) students. He explained that:

> When I was in year nine there was a thing for [name of elite university], where they like contacted our school to get ethnic minorities to go to the university, and you go for a whole week and stay there, sleep there, and it went over three years, and that kind of influenced me a lot to go to university, so it kind of worked backwards and influenced my sixth form choices. So rather than making me less likely to go, because of that thing it made me more likely to go. But I don't think it really does have that much of a difference because no matter where you are from nowadays you can still go to university. Because the opportunity is there mostly. I was in year nine, I just knew it was a university, I didn't know the status of it, or anything, so it was just like going to a school trip.

Jamal benefited from a programme aimed at increasing minority ethnic participation in elite universities. But the experience, which took place in year 9, had the effect of structuring some of his post-16 subject choices to enable him to proceed into higher education. Jamal would be the first in his family to participate so the programme proved useful to shift his habitus confirming Navarro's (2006: 16) claim that habitus 'is not fixed or permanent, and can be changed under unexpected situations or over a long historical period'. The unexpected situation of finding himself in an elite institution restructured his dispositions for the future towards the possibility of engaging in higher education.

In focus group three, there was some recognition that ethnicity plays a part in shaping experiences. This recognition was influenced by Ann and Adele's presence in the group. Both students are from African-Caribbean backgrounds and their ethnicity identity had influenced their post-18 decisions as discussed in Chapter 4. Sandra (white British, middle class) pointed out that:

> Yeah, to some extent, yeah, it does, because there are some careers you see like certain ethnic groups taking over different ethnic backgrounds and stuff, so I think that's important.

Sandra was aware that ethnicity could influence post-16 and post-18 pathways and subsequent career choices available. She reflected that certain ethnic groups dominate certain careers and that was an important factor in post-16 choices. Modood et al. (1997) highlight the way in which areas of work are dominated by different ethnicities, with very few minority ethnic individuals working in technology and the science careers.

The discussion related to ethnicity in focus group four was limited and focused on a rejection that it had any impact in the equal and meritocratic environment of the school. Similarly, in focus group five both Jen (white British, working class) and Paul (white British, working class) did not perceive their subject choices had been influenced by ethnicity either. They told me that:

> *Jen*:   Um, I don't think it's affected me in what I've chosen, because in my ICT class there's quite a lot of ethnicities, and it hasn't affected why I've decided to take it, so yeah, I don't think, and I don't think it does for a lot of people, I don't think, because it's such like a multicultural school.
>
> *Paul*:   I don't really think it has much effect on, definitely not on me, I didn't pick any choices because of ethnicity.

Jen acknowledges that the school is multicultural – however, white British students dominate the school. Again, the students who are both white British, struggle to understand the oppression and exclusion facing many minority ethnic young people as they navigate the British education system (Gillborn 2013).

The overwhelming response from the students in relation to the question – In what ways, if any, has ethnicity influenced your post-16 subject choices? – was a lack of recognition that there was any potential impact. There were some notable disruptions to this pattern as Jamal, Sandra and Julie were aware that there was some potential influence. The resistance to acknowledge any differences related to ethnicity from the majority of my participants highlight the potential problems still facing those students from a minority ethnic background. The potential issues include racialised subject choices and marginalisation of minority ethnic students' experiences within the formal school environment.

CONCLUDING REMARKS: POLICY, IDENTITY AND POST-16 PATHWAYS

This chapter has highlighted the ways in which policy changes and aspects of the participants' identities have influenced their post-16 choices in a range of complex, overt and hidden ways. The students had taken on the dominant discourse of Parkfield School, where the emphasis is on hard work and academic aspirations as the key to a successful future life. The teachers emphasised the meritocratic features of the school where anything was possible and believed that a student's identity was not a defining influence. The students seemed to overwhelmingly accept that individual success and failure rested in their hands and the future was a matter of working hard and aspiring to high status careers and success would follow. Gender, social class and ethnicity were not perceived by the majority of participants as a barrier to future success and many students talked about equality having been achieved. The influence of gender was strongly denied by almost all participants with the exception of focus group three, which was comprised of female only students. Perhaps the mixed focus groups made it harder for students to acknowledge that they had experienced gendered challenges or that gender had constrained their subject choices. The majority of students attending Parkside School are from economically privileged or economically comfortable families and perhaps this made it harder for those disadvantaged students I talked to, to acknowledge the barriers they might have faced to reach post-16 study. Many students in the focus groups similarly rejected ethnicity as an influential factor in their post-16 subject choices and aspirations for future careers. The overwhelming discourse was one of there's 'no problem here' (Gaine 1995).

The teachers and the students more easily acknowledged the policy context as an inhibiting influence although the responses were mixed with some students positively pleased that EMA had been removed, as it was perceived by many to be unfair and problematic, whilst others were dismayed that they had narrowly missed out on receiving these funds. The discussions relating to EMA revealed the pressure its removal had created for those disadvantaged students who needed to find funds in order to continue with their studies. All four students who missed out on EMA had to work long hours in part time jobs alongside studying for their A-levels, which contributed to them feeling tired and struggling to balance the demands of their studies with their paid employment.

The chapter has highlighted that policy changes alongside identity create favourable conditions for privileged, white students and places underprivileged students at a further disadvantage when compared to their peers. Chapter 4 builds on Chapter 3 and explores how the participants envisage they will navigate their post-18 choices and pathways.

Post-18 Educational Choices: 'Our Students Need to Avoid the easyJet Version of Universities'

INTRODUCTION

This chapter explores how the students decide upon their post-18 educational pathways in terms of the resources and support available to them from their teachers and families. I then explore how recent policy changes to higher education tuition fees have influenced the students' views on attending university and I provide the teachers' views on university as an option for their students' participation. Finally, I explore how the students' gender, social class and ethnicity influence their decisions to attend university and the type of university course and institution they intend to apply for. In examining their plans for their post-18 choices, I highlight any advantages possessed by those young people with more academically 'successful' identities in terms of their achievements. In this chapter I explore the following questions, focussing on the participants' post-18 plans to consider:

1. How have aspects of the participants' gender, social class and ethnicity influenced their decisions about their post-18 pathways?

---

eEasyjetEasyjet is an international, low cost budget airline that has been critiqued for its poor quality provision and poor standards of customer care. (Brignall and Timms 2015)

© The Author(s) 2017   79
K. Hoskins, *Youth Identities, Education and Employment,*
Policy and Practice in the Classroom,
DOI 10.1057/978-1-137-35292-7_4

2. How are the participants' choices and experiences influenced by the increase in university tuition fees?
3. How are the participants' plans for their post-18 pathways influenced by the current employment context?
4. How does the research cohort decide upon their post-16 and post-18 pathways given the resources and support available to them from their parents and teachers?

Planning University: The Role of the School and Teachers

In the focus group interviews with students I was keen to explore the key aspects that influenced their plans for the future. One of the central influences that they identified was the role played by the teachers and the Head of Post-16 Study in directing and influencing their post-18 plans towards university. It was no surprise then that the majority of the participants were intending to apply for university. The students' decision to apply to university was influenced by their family's aspirations, their own aspirations and also the aspirations held by the teachers in the school. The majority of the participants (17 of 22) explained that the teachers and Head of Post-16 Study are very keen on all students progressing to some form of university education. This aim and ambition for university was reflected in the sample as 18 of the 22 students were intending to participate in higher education. This ambition for higher education participation resonates with other research exploring post-18 aspirations (Wilkins and Burke 2014; Unterhalter et al. 2014) and reflects government policy agendas aimed at widening participation.

The aspiration for higher education participation guided the school's careers advice from the teachers, career advisors and senior leadership team. All of these members of staff were actively engaged in encouraging and guiding the students towards university. School staff were involved in multiple activities and initiatives including setting up visits to universities in the local vicinity, inviting university staff into the school to talk to the students about different fields of study and organising talks for the students about staff members' own experiences of university, emphasising their perceptions of the economic and social benefits conferred by a degree. In addition, the school's website provides details of the number of students planning to progress to university and also notes the number of those students applying to an elite Russell Group[1] university.

The school's institutional habitus was strongly orientated to academic progression, which is partly due to the school's historical examination success, but also resonates with the recent political ambitions for 50% participation in higher education during New Labour's office in government between 1997 and 2009 (Medway et al. 2003). In Bourdieu's (1993) terms, the field of this recently converted academy was circumscribed by the teachers' and school leaders' dispositions towards maximising higher education participation. Perhaps the school was keen for the students to attend university, partly due to the social and economic value conferred to the school through, for example, a strong position in national league tables that would enable them to maintain their predominantly middle-class intake.

The students described the influence of the school's aspiration for student higher education engagement as the norm, which is evident in the following data extracts:

> The school is mainly focused on the universities, so I find it harder to work out what I want to do, because they haven't said much. (Georgia, White British, working class)

> In form we had these UCAS books, and so many people were like 'I don't know if I want to go to uni', and my friend was like 'I'm not going to uni', and the teacher was like 'You have to go to uni, you have to fill it in', but my friend was like 'but I'm not going'. She's doing a BTEC in childcare... [...]. I feel like they are drumming it into us, and we don't have a choice. (Susie, White British, middle class)

> I want to go [to university] and get more education, like a degree, so I can get maybe like a better job, but I think teachers like drill it into you...because all we are talking about is universities, UCAS and stuff. (Jen, White British, working class)

> We did a higher education day, where basically we had the day off timetable and set up our UCAS applications, and talked about how to write a personal statement...And there was the option for you to go to the library and do like CVs, so they were trying to open it up for everyone, those who don't want to go to university, as well, but you might feel a bit left out of things here if you are not looking to go to university. (Paul, White British, working class)

These extracts highlight the pressure the students perceive they have experienced from the school and teachers to apply for university. The institutional habitus of the secondary school is shaped and influenced by the middle-class intake and this impacts on the aspirations for the future held by the students. Bourdieu (1990: 53) argues that:

> The conditionings associated with a particular class of conditions of existence produce habitus, systems of durable, transposable dispositions, structured structures predisposed to function as structuring structures, that is, as principles which generate and organize practices and representations that can be objectively adapted to their outcomes without presupposing a conscious aiming at ends or an express mastery of the operations necessary in order to attain them.

However, as Bourdieu and Wacquant (1992: 135) note 'it is only in the relation to certain structures that habitus produces given discourses or practices'. The students are experiencing the post-16 structures at Parkfield School, which are orientated towards higher education participation, partly due to the influence of the teachers' own university experiences and due to the school's history of successfully encouraging university participation, particularly in light of the wider context of policy changes.

Indeed, the students reported that the teachers are focused on ensuring as many students as possible attend some form of higher education. Even those students who are undecided about higher education, such as Georgia and Holly, indicated that, as far as advice from the teachers and school-based careers advisors was concerned, there are few alternative options. For example, Georgia told me that the careers advisors have very little advice on post-18 employment or apprenticeships:

> They said you can go and ask like the lady down the careers office about apprenticeships, but I just don't feel that there's much... It sort of feels they just say the same thing; 'you need to decide about higher education'. But I'm not sure if I want higher education. (Georgia, White British, working class)

The school's institutional habitus is focused on higher education participation and very little time and space is given to explore alternative pathways such as apprenticeships or employment.

Paul acknowledges that those students who are not planning to attend university as the next step could end up feeling left out of the higher education activities and discussions taking place in the school. The students acknowledged that there is little opportunity to explore apprenticeships, internships, vocational courses and non-graduate employment pathways. Stahl's (2015) research exploring the educational experiences and pathways available to white working-class boys revealed that his participants shared a similar sense of limited post-18 options. For those students not pursuing higher education, vocational education and training opportunities are scarce and typically fiercely competitive (Ainley and Allen 2010; European Union Committee 2012).

The students' ambivalence and uncertainty in relation to applying for university was acknowledged by four of the teachers, who were very aware of the pressure to encourage higher education participation. Maria told me that in her view:

> I've really noticed this academic year (2012/2013) how many students, by about November, December, hadn't decided if they are going to university and were really unsure about whether they want to do it or not. The uptake and applications are lower, and there is just this general feeling of uncertainty about whether university is something that they want to do; they are very much thinking about it more as a consumer than they would have done two years ago. (Maria, White British, Year 12/Post 16 Teacher)

From Maria's perspective, the significant increase in university tuition fees had contributed towards some of the students' sense of reluctance to pursue higher education. Parkfield School, with its below average intake of Free School Meal students and above average intake of economically secure students, had experienced a larger number of students intending to participate in higher education in previous years. The drop in university applications in 2012/2013 amongst Parkfield students was overwhelmingly attributed to higher education tuition fee increases. The concern about taking on substantial debt through higher education participation resonates with Wilkins et al.'s (Wilkins et al. 2013) research, which indicated that students are very concerned about the impact of student debt on their future lives. Students from working-class backgrounds are generally more debt adverse than their middle-class peers and display concerns about the risks of taking on debt when there are no guarantees of graduate employment (Wilkins et al. 2013).

John similarly acknowledged the pressure on students to pursue higher education at 18 years and he explained that this pressure was a source of stress and strain for many students:

> At the moment there's so much pressure, and if I'm honest I would probably say a bit of criticism of this school, as well, that, you know, we do get good results so we tend to be so focused on going to university, you must go to university...There's so much focus on it, and the students then become quite stressed with this...And some of them actually don't want to go to university, they don't know what to do at university so they haven't got the interest, and it's probably not right for them...and they are going to struggle. (John, White British, Head of Post 16 Study)

John's views raise some interesting and important ethical questions about whether university is the right choice for students. John was aware of several students who are applying to university due to limited alternative possibilities and their concerns about finding employment, which, as highlighted in Chapter 3, is extremely challenging. The requirement of a degree to gain many forms of skilled and professional employment has resulted in some young people attending university despite having no real desire to be there (Ainley and Allen 2010; Evans and Shen 2010). The issues related to non-graduate employment are further discussed in Chapter 5.

Julia was also unsure about the ethical dilemmas of encouraging the students at Parkfield School towards university, regardless of their academic ability, interests and ambitions for the future, because of a lack of alternative pathways. She told me that:

> I think we are kind of almost conning them, we are leading them on, and I think students actually are beginning to see it for themselves now, which is why they don't want to go to university. (Julia, White Irish, Year 12/Post 16 Teacher)

Julia's view highlights the ethical concerns expressed by all seven teachers about the impact created by widening participation in higher education. Not all students are suited to studying at university, but in the current context, there are relatively few vocational and employment alternatives (Ainley and Allen 2010). Indeed, the Higher Education Funding Council of England (HEFCE) is so committed to developing more apprenticeships, that is, has set up a '£1.6 million HEFCE Catalyst funding for higher apprenticeships in partnership with business' (Higher Education Funding Council for England (HEFCE) 2015). The key aim of the Catalyst fund is to 'develop a new education pathway for apprentices to continue their studies through foundation, bachelor and masters level' (Higher Education Funding Council for England (HEFCE) 2015). The establishment of the Catalyst fund acknowledges the need for more diverse post-18 provisions, but so far, demand has far exceeded supply (Higher Education Funding Council for England (HEFCE) 2015).

Daniel had a similar perspective to Julia about the ethical issues related to all of his students attending university, regardless of their suitability for higher education. Daniel was also concerned about the impact of increased tuition fees on higher education admissions. He told me that he had seen his students questioning the value of university education, particularly in light of the number of people who are unemployed, as youth unemployment remains a significant issue (Higher Education Statistics Agency (HESA) 2012). He explained that:

> I wonder if it's going to stop some people going to university, and if it's going to then segment the universities into just being the kind of middle class and above students who are going to go, and some other students will think 'well I can't afford it, my parents can't afford it'. (Daniel, White British, Year 12/Post 16 Teacher)

He felt that the issue of debt was significant to his less economically privileged students. They were, in his experience, the most likely group to express concern about accruing significant debt. Daniel cited the example of his own niece who was considering her post-18 options at the time of interview, and expressing concern about the level of debt she was facing. He told me that:

> My niece is thinking about going to university, she's in year twelve at the moment, and I know she's certainly worried and thinking 'how am I going to pay for my fees when I've finished my course? Am I going to be able to get a job?' And the job she wants to go and do isn't going to necessarily be the highest paid job, and that debt is an issue for her. (Daniel, White British, Year 12/Post 16 Teacher)

Daniel acknowledges and is troubled by the potential impact of them taking such significant amounts of debt, and he identifies the volume of debt as a key concern for some of his students. The programme of study and potential for future earnings associated with that programme are further concerns for Daniel and his students. Burke (2013), in her book arguing for the rights of all groups to participate and engage in higher education, contends that 'the willingness to accept debt as an inevitable part of the pursuit of "success" is tied to particular (white, middle class) values and dispositions' and thus 'detracts from wider questions about higher education as a public good'. The issue of taking on significant debt, and attitudes held by teachers and students towards debt was emphasised as a key concern.

The views of students and teachers in the sample highlight ambivalence towards higher education in a relatively advantaged school that would normally expect a significant proportion of students, up to 40–50% in previous years, to apply to university. My data introduces a challenge to Brown and Lauder (2012) argument that the credentialisation of many forms of employment and the pressure exerted by a skills based global economy will require increased levels of participation in higher education. If students are not prepared to accrue debt, then other pathways towards employment, such as apprenticeships or working up through a company, will be necessary. Students will be forced to draw on their extended networks to secure employment or perhaps take the decision to engage in distance learning through the Open University, which is a cheaper higher education option as tuition fees are approximately £5,500 per academic year (Open University 2016).

A glance at admissions figures to higher education in England over the last years, collected by the Independent Commission on Fees (ICoF), shows that admission rates did indeed drop in 2012 when the data for this study was collected, as the following table shows (Table 4.1):

The rates of university applications have increased by 1.3% between the 2013 academic year and the 2014 academic year according to the ICoF's

Table 4.1   Application rate (to March deadline) of 18-year-olds domiciled in England

	2010	2011	2012	2013	2014
England	31.3%	32.3%	30.8%	31.9%	33.2%

analysis (ICoF 2014, accessed November 2015). These admission rate increases suggest that despite an initial drop in higher education participation, the fee increases have not yet dissuaded large numbers of students from applying to university. Perhaps attendance rates have remained stable over the past 6 years because of the high youth unemployment rates, which peaked between 2012 and 2014 to over 1 million 16–24-year-olds (O'Neill 2016).

The perceptions of the students and teachers suggest real concerns about the impact of fee increases on any decisions to engage in higher education. My data reinforces the notion of students as consumers who seek out, with the help of their teachers (and parents as discussed below), the best course of study for their future, based primarily on the potential future economic return that certain pathways are more likely to yield. They also tend to seek work in sectors that are more 'recession proof' such as teaching, law and medicine. Many of the students considering university were also concerned about ensuring value for money, in terms of programme contact hours and supervisors' support, in light of the increases in tuition fees.

PLANNING TO ATTEND AN ELITE UNIVERSITY: VALUE FOR MONEY?

The school was not just focussed on getting students into any university. According to three of the students and all of the teachers, the school is 'very' focussed on getting as many pupils as possible into Russell Group institutions. In the previous academic year, the school website reported that approximately 50 students had applied for a Russell Group University in a cohort of 300 students, although the number of students that actually secured places at Russell group institutions was not reported on the website. The teachers and Head of Post-16 Study encouraged the students to aim high and these aspirations for maximising student entry into elite institutions is reflected in the students' discussions about where they were intending to apply:

> I want to go to a university in the Russell Group because the teachers told us that it kind of counts where you get your degree from. So I've kind of limited myself to applying for a Russell Group place on the school's advice. (Beth, White British, middle class)

> I'm looking at Russell Group unis, and I suppose I learnt that from school. They have a poster in the common room that has all of them on it, so yes,

higher education day and just hearing the teachers talking about it and things like that. (Tim, White British, middle class)

There were four students in the sample who were planning to apply to attend a Russell Group institution. These four students, two girls and two boys, were White and middle class. Tim and Beth described themselves as middle class and also both identified that they benefited from family support as their parents had first-hand experience of participation in higher education. These students' efforts to gain a place at a Russell Group university highlight the success of the targeted efforts made by the school to encourage students to aspire to participate in elite forms of higher education. The teachers had identified and supported the ablest students with their plans, but according to two of the teachers, this support had come at the cost of providing less support to those students who were not as sure about their future pathways and those pursuing more vocational pathways.

When I discussed the issue of applying to Russell Group universities with the teachers, it became clear that the aspiration for elite higher education participation was partly embedded in a value for money discourse. According to Maria:

> If you think about it Oxford and Cambridge are charging £9,000, and their student to staff ratio is so much lower than another university also charging £9,000. So a student approaching it as a consumer is thinking well I'm getting better value for money, where I sit with me and a lecturer two and three times a week. (Maria, White British, Year 12/Post 16 Teacher)

Maria, along with the other six teachers interviewed, was heavily invested in encouraging as many of her students as possible to apply to a Russell Group university. Her investment in elite higher education was based on a common sense approach that relates the cost of university tuition fees to the likely return on that investment in terms of future employment prospects. Reay et al.'s (Reay et al. 2005) research resonates with Maria's viewpoint; the authors found that particular schools encouraged and even directed students towards particular universities in keeping with the school's institutional habitus. David and Naidoo (David and Naidoo 2012) also note that schools attended by higher socio-economic status (SES) young people tend to provide extensive support and guidance about applying for university.

Jasper was similarly concerned about the issue of value for money offered by universities. In his view, the substantial increase in tuition fees meant that far more attention needed to be paid to the type of course and institution students pursue:

> Yeah, I mean I understand the political argument that maybe it's not affordable for it to be absolutely free...tax payers still pay into the higher education system and I can see the argument where there should be some contribution made by the student, I don't disagree with that. But it's where it finishes really. And all the predictions from the government that only a small percentage would be going up to the higher [fee] band has been proved wrong. It creates almost like this idea that the best universities will charge more, so I think there's going to be some kind of disproportionate weight put on universities that if you are charging nine grand it must be a good university, so I don't know where it leaves universities that charge three or four grand, that they are going to seem second tier, like the easyJet version of universities. I don't know really where it's going to go. And it's just worrying that once it starts I'm not sure where it stops. It's been a massive leap from three grand up to nine grand. (Jasper, white British, Year 12/Post 16 Teacher)

Jasper felt that Russell Group universities would charge the upper fee band. However, Jasper's prediction has not been borne out as in reality, the majority of English universities have been forced to charge the full £9,000 per annum for tuition fees for their undergraduate programmes, regardless of status differences between institutions and disciplines due to the rapid and substantial withdrawal of funding from the English government (Alcock 2011). Research by Bradley et al.'s (Bradley et al. 2013) Paired Peers project explored whether the respondents in their study felt their higher education represented value for money; very few students were satisfied with the return on the investment they had made. Students had calculated the costs of individual seminars/lectures and were not pleased if these were cancelled. However, students also noted the necessity of a degree to gain entry to many jobs and described the current context as 'a degree generation', where many semi-skilled jobs now require graduate level qualifications (Bradley et al. 2013: 10).

Jasper's notion of easyJet universities can be viewed as a symptom of the wider problem of the two-tier higher education system that exists in England (Hoskins 2012). The different status between 'old' and 'new' universities contributes to employability issues in terms of the value attributed to a degree from an elite institution compared with a new, post-1992 institution. Some of the top UK companies, for example the law firms Clifford Chance and Grant Thornton, are so concerned about the bias that exists in their recruitment processes in terms of where a candidate gained their degree that they have now introduced a 'university blind' recruitment strategy. The strategy requires candidates to blank out the university they attended so that their application cannot be discounted on the basis of their higher education (Policy Forum, November 2015).

PLANNING UNIVERSITY: COSTS AND CONCERNS

Set against the context of the financial commitment involved with gaining a degree, 17 of the 22 participants were intending to apply for a university place. They still constructed university as the opportunity and means to achieve their future occupational and professional dreams. They were generally aware of the fee increases and concerned about the impact of paying fees in terms of the financial pressure this could create for them in the future, but through rationalising strategies, they tended to push these worries about the financial pressures university would create to the back of their minds:

> It is a bad thing compared to paying £3,000 before, because £9,000 would pay for the whole course. But I think if you really want to go you shouldn't let that be a factor, I don't think you should think about that, if you want to do it I think you should do it anyway, regardless of whether the fees go up. (Sandra, White British, middle class)

> I suppose it's quite a negative, for me it's a lot of money, but we won't have to pay it back until we start working, so I suppose it's not too bad. (Jodie, White British, working class)

> I've been thinking about it, but I have to look at the long-run, that I'm going to get my degree at the end, so I have to be positive about it, not look at the fees, but just look at the long-run, like my career, and don't think about the money side too much. (Ann, Black African-Caribbean, working class)

> I know it's a lot of money, but if you want to do it then it's worth it. (Laura, White British, middle class)

These participants, who self-identified as a mixture of working and middle class, felt that whilst university attendance was going to be expensive it was also going to be worth it and important and necessary to secure a high status and professional career. They put the fees to the back of their minds as their student debt would not be payable for some time and they focussed on the benefits that they believed a university education would confer. These students were all considering where to apply and how far away from home they wanted to travel. Perhaps, similar to Callender and Jackson's (2008: 426) respondents, these young people were:

> much more willing to respond to fear of debt by living near their family home and pursuing a course in the subject they wanted, rather than to change the subject or the type of course they wanted to pursue.

A couple of the participants, who were both applying to Russell Group universities, conceptualised the level of debt as similar to taking on a mortgage, and thus, a necessary and measured risk. Adrian told me that:

> It's a similar debt to if you have a mortgage...it's not really a debt at all. (Adrian, White British, middle class).

Adrian is from a privileged family background and perhaps this has enabled him to conceptualise student debt as necessary to enable him to achieve his future potential. Adrian's attitude towards debt resonates with Burke's (2013: 139) claim that accepting 'debt as an inevitable part of the pursuit of 'success' is tied to particular (White, middle class) values and dispositions'. Therefore, Burke (2013) suggests that attitudes towards debt relate to 'certain social groups' position in the labour market', with those able to secure a university place on a programme that will lead to professional and high status future occupations better positioned to take on high levels of student debt.

However, two participants had wanted to attend university, but had been put off by the significant increase in university tuition fees and questioned the value and worth of a degree. Holly (white British, unsure of class background/probably middle class) had wanted to improve her career potential for the future, but was not prepared to take on the high levels of debt required to achieve her goal. Stephanie (white British, middle class) was similarly not sure about attending university because of the risks associated with accruing high levels of debt. These views provide some evidence of disposition disruption in these participants' choices as both Stephanie and Holly are from what could be described as middle-class families on the basis of their parents' occupations and in these families university attendance was the norm, yet they were choosing not to attend, partly because of their concerns about managing the debt and the value for money conferred by degree status.

The data discussed here reveals that all of the students who intended to apply for higher education, regardless of the institution they were applying to, were extremely strategic in their discussions about which institutions they would apply to and on what basis they would apply. They displayed a keen sense of value for money and had high expectations for their under-graduate programmes of study and expected high quality teaching and learning provision and pastoral as well as academic support. This is consistent with research findings by Host (Swain 2012) whose research found that students expect and demand high quality teaching and learning. Set against the neoliberal further and higher education context in England, the students I interviewed are, without exception, driven by consumer concerns including value for money, quality and quantity of provision. They are skilful at accessing information about the higher education programmes they are interested in applying to through school based resources, particularly their well-educated teachers who are central to supporting and guiding their efforts.

PLANNING UNIVERSITY: FAMILY EXPECTATIONS AND INFLUENCES

The school and the teachers were not the only key influences on the students' plans for higher education participation; participants talked about the important role that their families had played in their decision to apply for university. Many talked of supportive parents who helped them to think carefully about their choice of university and course. The influence of their familial habitus was evident in their talk about family expectations for university:

> My mum really influenced my choice [to apply for university]; she was like look at your strengths and what you think you'll be like be best at, and she's very interested in a lot of things, so she sort of guided me where she thought I'd fit in. (Claudia, White British, middle class)

> I want to go and get more education, like a degree, so I can get maybe like a better job, but I think parents like drill it into you, because all we are talking

about is universities, UCAS and stuff. I think it's very much to do with family expectations for me. (Jen, White British, working class/middle class)

Going to university has always kind of been drilled into me by my family. So it's like you are going to sixth form, you are getting your A levels, going to uni, and you are getting a good job. (Julie, White British, middle class)

These extracts highlight the influence of family expectations and aspirations. Parents and families are central to these students' decision-making processes and should not be underestimated as they are by the UK government (Hoskins and Barker 2014). Despite government education policies, for example the 2010 White Paper (HM Government 2010), which stated its key aim was to enable children to overcome their family background and unleash their individual (economic) potential regardless of their identity, the influences and familial advice provided by parents, siblings and extended members remains central to many young people (Hoskins and Barker 2014). The students are from both working- and middle-class backgrounds and hold aspirations for diverse careers. These examples suggest that the influence of family cuts across social class categorisations and plans for future career pathways, highlighting the centrality of the family in the participants' plans for their future.

When Susie reflected on why she was applying to university she was unable to articulate her exact motivations. But she identified the influence of her mother's recent divorce from her father as a defining factor:

I don't actually know why I want to go to uni, it's just my family have always pushed it. My mum didn't go to uni and when she was with my dad she never had to work, she never had a full-time proper job. Now she's studying to do the Knowledge, to be a black cab driver. Since her and my dad haven't been together she's always been like Susie you have to do well at school, she's sort of like drummed it into my head, because she doesn't want me to be like how she was. [...] So I just thought it was the thing that you should do, you didn't have the choice. I think it's always been in my head to go. (Susie, white British, middle class)

The intersection of gender with social class is apparent in Susie's story. Susie explained that her mother had experienced financial hardship as a consequence of separating from her father and this hardship had impacted on the advice she was providing to her daughter. Susie's mother was keen that her daughter should become financially independent in the future to avoid ending up in the situation she found herself in – training for her first job 'full time proper job' in her late forties.

These four female students identified their parents, and particularly their mothers, as an important factor in their decision to apply to university. Despite their different class backgrounds –that is, Claudia, Susie and Julie are middle class and Jen is working/middle class – their durable dispositions, inculcated through their family habitus, are influenced by an aspiration to gain higher education. The influence of mothers on their children's aspirations has been noted in existing literature exploring educational choice-making processes (see, e.g., Ball et al. 2000; Archer et al. 2010). My earlier research similarly found that working-class and middle-class parents, particularly mothers, were an important factor in their daughters' educational aspirations and decision-making processes, particularly in relation to post-16 and post-18 pathways (Hoskins and Barker 2014). Vincent and Ball's (2007: 1061) research highlighted the 'parental strategies for class reproduction' pursued by middle-class parents, which started when their children were pre-schoolers, and continued throughout their education, in an attempt to ensure their children's future privilege. A key strategy for middle-class parents involved ensuring their children were able to access high status university courses. Thus, the family is central to some of the participants' planning processes. These young people were shaped by their family habitus in terms of their future horizons for action and their choices for the future which are circumscribed by the form of social capital available to them (Hoskins and Ball 2017).

PLANNING UNIVERSITY: DOING IT FOR YOURSELF

The last theme relating to planning university was those participants who were aspiring and applying using their own initiative, with limited support from their family or teachers. Three of the participants (Jodie, Paul and Ann) talked about the importance of wanting to gain a degree to improve their employment prospects for the future, even though their families and the school were not pushing them towards higher education. They all expressed desire and motivation to attend, evidenced in the following quotations:

> Neither of my parents went to uni, and I think when I'm in school, sixth form, a lot of us talk about university and things, and even though some people might feel there's pressure from the school I think you've got to want

to do it yourself, and I think I decided I wanted to go when I started sixth form. I decided like, what I wanted to study, and before then I didn't really know what I wanted to go into, and so I didn't want to go to uni just to get a degree and then not have a job relating to that. And so I decided what I wanted to do, decided I wanted to go and study and that would help me with work. (Jodie, White British, working class)

I want to go to uni for myself and to improve my job opportunities, and in general you need a degree to get better sort of jobs nowadays, but neither of my parents have been to university, so they weren't like drilling it in that you have to go. (Paul, White British, working class/middle class)

I've always been independent, I don't like to rely on my parents or anything, so I saw university as an independency, to broaden me, I would say, and also really focus on my career for myself. So like, from GCSEs, I always thought to myself I'm going to go to uni, I'm going to get good grades, I don't want to rely on no one, yeah, pretty much I would say. (Ann, Black African-Caribbean, working class)

These three students are all from working-class families and would be the first in their families to attend higher education. Their families were broadly supportive of their plans to participate in higher education, but they had limited knowledge of how higher education systems work. The students' motivation to attend university was based on their own desire to improve their future employment prospects and rooted in their sense of personal agency. Part of their motivation was linked to these three participants' experiences of economic hardship at home, and their determination to avoid experiencing anything similar in their own future lives. A further element of this agentic desire to participate was to enable them to become more independent from their parents, to live their own lives and make their own choices. These participants described themselves as academically competent and independent, themes that resonate with Crozier and Reay (2011) research exploring how working-class students learn how to navigate higher education. Crozier and Reay (2011) found that some of their working-class participants had a positive sense of their own successful learner identity and were independent and confident when they arrived at university, highlighting the diversity of working-class experience.

The data highlight that social class, alongside gender and ethnicity, influence how young people choose the future in myriad ways. To elaborate this discussion, I now explore if and how social class, gender and ethnicity influenced the participants' post-18 choices, in terms of the programme of study they intended to pursue. The following section explores how identity shaped the participants' choice of university course.

IDENTITY AND UNIVERSITY COURSES

To better understand decisions about university, I questioned the participants about the course they wanted to apply for and asked them to reflect on if and how they perceived that social class, gender and ethnicity had influenced their choices. I wanted to understand how the intersections between these aspects of the participants' identities had shaped their decisions about the subject they were intending to study. The students had all attended sixth form sociology lectures; therefore, they were familiar with the terminology of social class, gender and ethnicity. The majority of participants were adamant that they are autonomous and agentic choosers and are not constrained or influenced by their identity in any way. Indeed, as outlined in Chapter 3, their responses to questions about the possible impact of identity on their pathways were very much there's 'no problem here' (see Gaine 1995).

However, as I argued in Chapter 3, on closer analysis it was possible to infer that the participants' identities had played a significant role in guiding their choices for the future and this role was evident in some of the discussion about their plans for university. Whilst there are several areas where identity could be a determining factor in their future plans, in this section I focus on the area of study they hoped to pursue and the type of institution they planned to attend.

Identity and University Courses: The Influence of Gender

Taking gender first, 18 of the participants are female and there was evidence that gender had impacted on the sorts of courses and institutions some of the students were planning to apply for. For example, several of the girls wanted a future career in either teaching, social work or sociology and this aspiration cut across the participants' social-class background with both middle-class and working-class female students hoping to pursue these so-called feminised areas of study and future employment. Jodie, Julie, Sandra and Laura had aspirations to become primary school teachers and were all applying for BA Education Studies programmes at various English universities. Kim was planning to become an English Language secondary school teacher in the future and this pathway, she explained, would enable her to work and travel as her qualifications would provide her with the possibility of becoming an English as an Additional Language (EAL) teacher in the future. The following quotations evidence Julie's and Sandra's aspirations to complete a BA Education degree:

> I do want to go to uni, it's always something I've wanted to do personally, but then like the teachers said you have to have a degree if you want to compete to get a job, and for what I want to do as well, I need a degree as I want to be a teacher. I'm not sure if my gender has influenced my desire to teach. (Julie, White British, middle class)

> Because teaching is a very female sort of job, there's loads of females, like in primary school all of my teachers were female, and as I want to move on and teach I think that might have influenced me to studying teaching. (Sandra, White British, middle class)

The demographic figures for the teaching profession reveal that across primary and secondary education 'out of the 365,000 teachers in England, 74% are female' (Welham 2014), thus it was perhaps normalised that these female participants aspired to become teachers. The General Teaching Council for England (GTCE) (2011) data suggests that 88% of primary school teachers are female, highlighting the greater percentage of women who teach younger children and thus the stronger association with females as caring. Both Julie and Sandra were unsure about the influence of their gender on their decision to study teaching at university, but as Sandra noted, the high proportion of female teachers is a likely influence on her aspiration formation.

Susie expressed her commitment and determination to become a social worker, borne out of her desire to help others and make a positive difference in her working life:

> I know what I want to do and I don't need any help with it, because for years, years and years and years, I've always like wanted to be a social worker... Like my auntie's a social worker, so she's told me what I need to have and what I need to do, so that hasn't changed.

Similar to teaching, social work is an overwhelmingly feminised profession and 'over 75% of qualified social workers in England are female' (Galley 2014). Cree (2013) notes that social work has long been acknowledged by feminists as women's work, partly because of the caring and nurturing overtones that underpin the profession. Indeed, the desire to make a positive difference through caring and nurturing is a prominent theme, well documented in the literature (see, e.g., Skelton and Francis 2009). Susie's desire to become a social worker can also be read as an example of gendered social reproduction as her auntie was a social worker and had encouraged Susie to pursue the profession. Susie's dispositions, which were inculcated in early childhood, have arguably generated 'practices and perceptions' (Bourdieu 1993: 5), which inclined her to choose social work.

Beth articulated her desire to become a psychologist in her adult life and began by commenting that psychology was probably quite a female dominated area of work. However, she went on to explain that her gender had not influenced her to study this subject:

> I'm going to study psychology. I guess that's kind of more girls would do psychology than guys maybe, but I find it the most interesting subjects so I want to go and do it.

Beth rejected my probing that perhaps gender might have influenced her choice to study psychology and told me that:

> I don't really think gender affects it really... it's just something that I want to study... I don't think gender really comes into it, to be honest. I think nowadays there's such a big emphasis on equality that it's almost been eradicated from the whole system. I don't think there's any preferential treatment or discrimination. (Beth, White British, middle class)

Beth's rejection of gendering in her education provides some evidence of what Francis (2000: 141) has described as the 'innate equality' discourse between boys and girls, which is evoked by pupils to deconstruct the 'gender dichotomy' between boys and girls. Innate equality is a way of 'presenting the genders as the same' and was used by Francis's (2000: 141) participants who argued that 'people are the same regardless of their gender'. I encountered the innate equality discourse from Beth, and also from Julie who desired a career in teaching but resisted constructing her aspiration for teaching as gendered.

These examples of career aspirations also resonate with Francis's (2000) work exploring the construction of gendered identities and gendered subjectivities. Francis argues that our choices are constrained by dominant discursive constructions of what is gender 'appropriate' behaviour and she suggests that gendered aspirations and plans for the future enable young people to 'do' gender in ways that feel more comfortable for them. These ways of doing gender reinforce and normalise particular horizons for action as gender appropriate and in so doing, limit the range of possible positions young people can experience without penalty from their peers (Francis 2000). My participants had experienced dominant gender discourse in relation to their subject and career choices, despite their denial of these influences.

Identity and University Courses: The Influence of Ethnicity

Ethnicity was also a key influence on some of the participants' plans for the subject they intended to study at university, for example, the experiences of Ann and Adele, who are both from African-Caribbean families. Ann was planning to study clinical psychology and Adele was intending to study medicine. Both students constructed higher education success as the key to unlocking their future lives. However, both participants talked of experiencing inequality as a result of their ethnic identity. Ann and Adele explained that they had experienced in and out of the school racial discrimination and this had motivated them to strive to achieve high status and professional careers. Both students were aware they needed to pursue high status university courses in terms of subject area to achieve a high status career. Ann (Black African-Caribbean, working class) told me that:

> Being black has affected me a little bit, because I knew that I'd have to work harder for things.

Adele (Black African-Caribbean, middle class) agreed with Ann's sentiment and explained that in her experience, her ethnicity has similarly meant that she perceives that she has to work harder:

> We have to work harder because we are black, so you want people to see that you are working hard to get what you want, but for some ethnic groups it's so much easier to break into some areas of work. I understand what she's saying; if you want to achieve something you have to strive for it, and don't let the ethnicity get in the way.

Ann's claim that she, along with other black students, has to work harder because of her ethnicity is confirmed in the entry to higher education statistics (Basit and And Modood 2016). The authors draw on Croxford and Raffe (2014) to argue that minority ethnic students are more likely to gain offers for university through clearing, but to new, less prestigious institutions rather than older, Russell Group universities. Basit and Modood (2016) also note that there are considerable differences related to minority ethnic groups, with Chinese students receiving far more offers than Black African and Black Caribbean students.

In terms of degree subject choice, Codiroli (2015: 4) argued that this is an under researched area, but the limited existing research points to disparities in subject choice:

> For A-level choices, Black Caribbean students are least likely to study STEM subjects given their prior attainment, and White British students have particularly low uptake of Math (Boaler, Altendorff and Kent, 2011). Considering students from Black and Minority Ethnic (BME) backgrounds also tend to have lower academic attainment as well as more deprived social backgrounds, it is likely diversity will increase when these characteristics are controlled.

Codiroli (2015) argues that minority ethnic students are less likely to study high status subject areas. To address the disparity of access to high status universities and reified programmes of study experienced by some groups of minority ethnic students, legislation has been introduced that demands institutions to publish their admissions by ethnicity (Wright 2015). The stories of Ann and Adele highlight how their ethnic identity and experiences of racism had motivated them to work hard to secure places on university courses that could provide them with the opportunities to move into professional and secure careers.

In contrast, Kim (Chinese, working class) felt that her ethnicity was not a factor in her future plans. She told me that:

> I don't think ethnicity has influenced my plans for the future, I just don't think the colour of my skin has changed what I want to do, I want to be a teacher and that's that.

Whilst describing her family background as working class, Kim's ethnic background is Chinese which, according to Basit and Modood (2016), would mean that Kim is statistically better placed to access higher education than her Black Caribbean peers. Later in the focus group, Kim expanded her answer further and told me that whilst she did not feel her ethnicity had marginalised her from her higher education programme of study, it had contributed to a sense of responsibility to 'pay back' her parents' investment in her education:

> I don't think my ethnicity would matter in terms of uni applications, but I feel a lot more pressure to make the money that my parents invested to let me go to the UK, and keep me in education this long, I feel that I need to sort of make that worthwhile in a way, so go to a good uni and get a good degree. But I don't think that my background really affects any of my choices. (Kim, Chinese, working class)

Kim's sense of needing to ensure she delivers a return on her parents' investment in her education is clear here. She is ambivalent about the way her ethnicity has shaped her choices. The examples of Ann, Adele and Kim emphasise the nuanced differences that exist in relation to ethnicity, aspiration and achievement in the English education system and show that more could be done to ensure that all students, regardless of social identity, have an opportunity to engage with high status subject areas.

When I asked the students about their views on the possible influence of ethnicity on their choice of university course, those from white British backgrounds all stated that ethnicity was not a factor. The following quotes highlight two of the white British participants' sense that racial equality prevails:

> I don't really notice how my ethnicity affects what I've done. I don't think it really, it really matters at all, in terms of like especially applying for university, they see your grades and your name, and they don't necessarily know what ethnicity you are before they even consider you. I don't think that's really factored into university applications. And like I said before, everyone has the same opportunities as each other, so I don't think that really is something that is an advantage or disadvantage anymore. (Beth, White British, middle class)

> I agree with what Beth said, we are so multicultural in this school ... I think it's normal for us now to do anything, it's changed a lot, so I don't think now it really matters what ethnic group you belong to and stuff. (Adrian, White British, middle class)

These students had not experienced any marginalisation or inequality as a consequence of their ethnic identity and perhaps for this reason, they could not understand and empathise with the challenges associated with being minority ethnic in an overwhelmingly white society.

However, there was some disruption to this limited acknowledgement of the role of ethnicity in choosing university subjects. Claudia (White British, middle class), provided the following, more tentative response:

> I don't know, I think we are pretty equal, because we have got such a broad ethnicity at this school, but I think we don't all get like the same level of support…I don't know, like the meetings for like higher graded students, so some people are getting less help, and they are not getting…like for Oxbridge candidates who don't even want to apply there they are getting extra help with their personal statements and all that kind of thing, so it makes it more competitive for other people who want to apply to the Russell Groups that aren't Oxford or Cambridge, so it really lessens their chances, they are going to have a much weaker personal statement, but I don't know if, I don't know how ethnicity comes into it exactly.

Those minority ethnic students who are academically capable are encouraged by the teachers at Parkfield School to work on producing high quality personal statements to increase their chances of securing a place at an elite university, regardless of whether they intended to apply. Claudia was unsure about how ethnicity shaped the support process, but had some awareness that it did make a difference. Shiner and Noden (2014: 1188) in their study exploring BME access to higher education found that 'schooling plays a pivotal role in higher education choice, simultaneously facilitating and constraining the choices available to candidates'. Those schools who supported their students' applications, predominately independent schools and high performing state schools, encouraged and supported BME students to apply for places at elite institutions and to study elite subject areas (Shiner and Noden 2014). This form of positive discrimination approach was used at Parkfield to maximise student participation in higher education.

The role and influence of ethnicity in shaping university subject choices is complex and nuanced and depends on each participant's own ethnic identity and experiences. The students from BME groups were more likely to have experienced inequality as a consequence of their ethnicity than those students from white backgrounds. This inequality had made Ann and Adele more determined to secure places on high status university courses to enable them to achieve high status careers in the future.

Identity and University Courses: The Influence of Social Class

The impact of social class in terms of university course applied for was less of a factor than gender and ethnicity in my data, but nevertheless, social class had influenced several of the participants' plans for university, evidenced in their discussions about the courses they intended to study. Those participants aiming to get A or A* A-level results and apply for high status courses at Russell Group institutions were White, British and middle class. They talked about their plans for university with confidence. They were strategic in their approach to selecting courses and institutions that matched their ambitions for adult life. Their identities and habitus are in-keeping with much of the literature and stereotypes about the sorts of people who aspire to, and gain access to, an elite higher education (Crozier and Reay 2011). They had all identified that anything less than Russell Group would not be 'for the likes of us' (Bourdieu 1990: 77). For example, Tim (White British, middle class) was applying to study biochemistry and Adrian (White British, middle class) was applying to study mathematics.

In the following exchange some of the students in focus group four (all of whom are White British and middle class) explained to me why they were applying to Russell Group institutions only:

Adrian: Class hasn't affected me as such, but there's obviously a lot of pressure to get into the top unis, and make your parents proud, I guess. I don't know, I'm just going to see how it goes and get into whatever.

Tim: I want to go to a uni in the Russell Group, because it kind of counts where you get your degree from ... So I've kind of limited myself to Russell Group, and then the courses, student happiness, and like yeah ...

KH: And did you know about Russell Group because of parents, or school, where does that knowledge come from?

Beth: We had a higher education evening a while ago, and we had all the uni open days, open evening, that sort of thing ...

Adrian: Yeah, same with me, I'm looking at Russell Group unis, and I suppose I learnt that from school. They have a poster in the common room that has all of them on it, so yes, higher education day and just hearing the teachers talking about it and things like that.

As discussed in Chapter 3, the teachers at Parkfield are focussed on ensuring that as many students as possible attend university and preferably a high status Russell Group institution. For Beth, Tim and Adrian, who are all White British and from middle-class families, there is an expectation that they will attend a high status institution. This example points towards social reproduction for these students as they all come from privileged families and were under pressure to maintain that privilege. These students all shared a middle-class habitus where participation at an elite university was an expectation from their respective families.

The majority of my participants had thought and planned their next steps extensively and in strategic ways. Most of the students in the sample were intent on pursuing higher education and had very firm expectations and ideas about what that would entail. They were clear about what they expected from these institutions and the sorts of careers they intended to get out of their degrees. However, a minority in the sample were very unclear about their next steps and they were planning to wait and see what their results would bring them. They thought employment was their most likely next step because of the associated costs of university participation; their stories are discussed in Chapter 5.

CONCLUDING REMARKS: CHOOSING UNIVERSITY: WIDENING PARTICIPATION AND SOCIAL JUSTICE CONCERNS

As discussed in Chapter 2, recent policy changes resulting in significant increases to the costs of higher education have become an important factor in the decision-making process for the participants intending to apply for university at the end of their compulsory education. University tuition fees in England have increased from £3,300 per annum in 2011–2012 to an average of £8,500–£9,000 as of September 2012. There are financial arrangements in place to ensure that students do not have to pay back the loans they have accrued to cover fees and living expenses during their time at university until they are working and earning more than £21,000 per annum. The loan will be deducted directly from the individual's wages along with tax and national insurance so the participants will not be responsible for making payments. However, despite these financial arrangements, the increase in tuition fees is a challenge to the widening participation in higher education agenda as it raises social justice questions about which students will no longer identify university as a realistic option for them and which students will continue to pursue a degree. Burke's (2012) research explored those students who participate and those who tend to self-exclude from higher education on the basis of a range of factors including an individual's social class background, economic wealth and social resources. Burke (2012) argues that higher education is a right for all, but acknowledges that realising this right is deeply problematic, partly due to the financial costs of participation.

Similarly, Wilkins et al. (2013: 136) found that 'the increase in tuition fees in England in October 2012 will likely affect students' study choices'. They found that a quarter of their respondents were 'considering post-poning university studies and almost one-fifth considering cheaper higher education options' (Wilkins et al. 2013: 136). This evidence resonates with my findings as several of my participants were considering not apply-ing for higher education on the basis of fee increases.

The data presented and analysed in this chapter concurs with the findings of numerous other research projects exploring the intersectional effects of identity on the individual. For example, research by Reay et al. (2005) illustrates the degrees of higher education participation and choice, arguing the New Labour expansion of HE has significantly increased social stratification. Vignoles et al. (2008: 1) provided quanti-tative analysis of 'Widening Participation in Higher Education'. This analysis developed a 'theoretically based quantitative empirical analysis of the higher education experience of different students, particularly disadvantaged students, ethnic minorities, women, those entering HE without A levels and mature students'. The research concluded, amongst other things, that 'policy interventions on disadvantaged pupils who are already in post-compulsory education are unlikely to have a serious impact on the socio-economic gap in HE participation' (Vignoles et al. 2008: 6). Fuller et al. (2006) explored issues around non-participation in HE and argued that decision making is an embedded social practice and is dependent on an individual's 'networks of intimacy' consisting of family members and close friends in relation to the participants' HE choices. The tuition fee increases since these three studies were published have only compounded the challenges facing non-traditional students as evidenced by Wilkins et al. (2013).

The data presented in this chapter reveals some interesting areas worthy of further study. First, the decision by some of the middle-class participants not to progress to university, because of the increase in the top-up fees and the long-term financial implications of these. This could also indicate a shift in the values and aspirations of some sections of the middle classes. For example, perhaps those described in the BBCs (BBC Science 2013) new class schema as Emergent service workers, the category described as 'a new, young, urban group which is relatively poor but has high social and cultural capital' could find university a less viable pathway in the future. The value of university in relation to the employment market is certainly changing, fuelled in part by mainstream media representations of an overpriced sector which often falls short of delivering a recompense return. Such a view is borne out in a recent study showing that universities emphasise securing students and put less effort into the student experience once term beings (Doward and Ratcliffe 2016). Set against this context, it is not surprising some of the young people in this study displayed ambivalence towards higher education. They were not convinced a degree would deliver job security and future financial compensation commensurate to the immediate risks associated with high levels of debt, despite all sorts of reassurances from government, the school and the teachers about the terms of repayment (Wilkins et al. 2013). Rather, they intend to draw on their social capital networks to gain entry to their chosen career pathway and work their way up, a strategy that is discussed in Chapter 5.

A second area of interest relates to these young people's expectations for the quality they hoped to gain from participating in higher education. All of the students who were intending to apply for some form of higher education were extremely strategic in their discussions about which institutions they would apply for and why and this decision-making rested on their perceptions about which institutions would deliver an economic return. They displayed a keen sense of value for money and had high expectations for their undergraduate programmes of study and expected high quality teaching and learning provision. The teachers at Parkfield and many of the parents were reinforcing these high expectations. This attitude towards higher education is consistent with research findings released by Host (Swain 2012) who found that students expect high quality teaching and learning, partly through high levels of contact hours and extensive tutor support. The participants' talk about university indicated the extent to which they approach their higher education decisions as consumers, seeking to translate the economic investment in their higher education into suitable professional employment. Value for money was a key concern for these participants, and their parents and teachers encouraged them to fully explore their options and strive for an offer for a high status programme at the most prestigious university they could achieve.

A third area to explore relates to degree value. Are the majority of high performing state comprehensive schools such as Parkfield School all encouraging students to seek out a more elite Russell Group university education? The teachers and senior leaders I interviewed were all encouraging the more academically able students towards applying for Russell Group institutions, citing the benefits of an elite degree in the employment market and also their intention to enhance their school's reputation. Over time, this sort of push could have a significant impact on newer, less prestigious universities, particularly if fees are to remain broadly the same for all institutions and all subject areas, although the incoming Teaching Excellence Framework (TEF) is likely to reshape the higher education fee landscape significantly. According to Bishop (2016: 1) the key aims of the TEF are:

> To help students select courses, to increase access of under-represented groups to higher education, to provide a basis for allowing universities to raise fees, and to provide criteria for 'new entrants' (ie, private institutions) that wish to enter the higher education market.

As such, the fees charged for courses are likely to change and fees could become relational to the subject area and to the reputation of individual institutions.

Not all of the students intended to continue with their education. Some expressed ambitions for work or trying to find an apprenticeship to earn and learn, as they felt they had studied enough and needed a change. The next chapter explores the experiences of those participants seeking employment when they left school. I consider the strategies and approaches they intended to employ to secure suitable employment, which includes access to networks through their parents' contacts and ambitions for a life beyond an education system that did not speak to their aspirations for their adult lives.

NOTE

1. Russell Group universities are often described as '"elite". The 24 institutions – which include Oxford, Cambridge, Durham, Manchester and Warwick – carry out some of the most highly rated research in the world and have a reputation for academic excellence' (Ratcliffe 2012).

Alternative Possibilities and Pathways: Youth Employment and Apprenticeships in a Graduate World

INTRODUCTION

In this chapter I explore the alternative pathways available to those students in my cohort who are not applying to university. The alternative pathways discussed in the focus groups and interviews included apprenticeships and possibilities for gaining non-graduate employment. Drawing on Lanning and Rudiger (2012), the chapter explores whether their claim that 'young people in the UK are largely left to navigate the transition to work and responsible adulthood alone, and the support they receive varies wildly across different families, communities and employers' is relevant in relation to the experiences of those participants not intending to proceed into higher education. I also analyse the teachers' views about the forms of support available to those students not applying to university.

Since university tuition fees tripled in 2012, the value of a degree has come under considerable scrutiny from parents, students and employers. A recent dataset entitled Longitudinal Education Outcomes (LEO) (2016) found that:

> the median earnings for a graduate were £16,500 one year on from when they left university in 2004, increasing to £22,000 after three years and rising to £31,000 in 2014. The lowest quartile of graduate earners fared significantly worse. A year after they graduated in 2004 their median earnings were just £11,500, rising to £16,500 after three years and £20,000 after 10.

© The Author(s) 2017
K. Hoskins, *Youth Identities, Education and Employment*,
Policy and Practice in the Classroom,
DOI 10.1057/978-1-137-35292-7_5

In contrast, young people who had pursued an apprenticeship with, for example, Jaguar Land Rover were earning around £30,000 and had not incurred high levels of debt associated with higher education (Longitudinal Education Outcomes 2016). The issue of debt was a key part of the participants' decision-making processes in terms of their post-18 pathways.

The discussion of alternative pathways directly related to four participants who did not intend to apply for a university place and were instead considering their employment options. However, the majority of the student participants had views about the possible advantages and disadvantages of seeking employment or an apprenticeship once they completed their schooling at the age of 18. The teachers also held strong views about the need for recognition of vocational qualifications and aspirations, noting that not all young people are suited to university. In what follows I explore the employment plans and alternative pathways discussed by participants. This chapter addresses research questions 1 and 3:

1. How have aspects of the participants' gender, social class and ethnicity influenced their decisions about their post-18 pathways?
3. How are the participants' plans for their post-16 and post-18 pathways influenced by the current employment context?

Employment Plans: Precarity and Uncertainty

Those students intending to pursue employment had wanted to participate in university, but they were put off by the significant increase in university tuition fees and they questioned the value and worth of a degree (Wilkins et al. 2013). Perhaps their disengagement from applying to university explains why the students seeking employment seemed vague about the sort of employment they would pursue once they completed their further education. As discussed in Chapter 4, the teachers and students at Parkfield School felt that very little effort was made at the school for those students not intending to apply to university.

Holly (white British, unsure of class background, probably middle class) was perhaps the most undecided participant and had not ruled out university, but she thought it was highly unlikely she would attend. She explained that:

No, I'm not sure. I might go to uni, but I never wanted to go. But it's because everyone's talking about it now, making me want to go a little bit, but it's very expensive, I don't want the debt for the rest of my life. So I just really don't know what to do. (Holly, White British, unsure of class background/probably middle class)

Later in the focus group Holly elaborated on her concerns regarding university participation and explained her reluctance to take on degree debt:

I think you need to think more carefully about what degree you are going to take now, because most people are just going to like do a degree, and get the experience, but now there's so much more you have to think about than just the degree to get a good job.

Holly showed awareness of the need for extra-curricular activities and experiences alongside gaining a degree in order to be employable. Brooks (2007) has shown that young people are very aware of the need to volunteer and highlights the complex reasons that motivate young people to engage with volunteering, including, but not limited to, improving their employability prospects. Holdsworth (2010: 434) similarly found from her survey research with 3,083 young people, that they were motivated to volunteer to strengthen their employability potential, but they were also motivated by a range of other more nuanced, altruistic reasons such as a sense of 'synergies between different volunteering experiences and how volunteering was integral to their transitions to adulthood'. Holly's comment that there is so much more than just a good degree to consider to ensure graduate employment was perhaps a reflection of the social and economic context framing her experiences. The percentage of youth unemployment at the time of Holly's interview was at its highest in recent times at 14.4% (Boffey 2015), which might have contributed to her sense of precarity about the possibility of gaining graduate employment. Holly, like Jamal, had applied for many low-skilled jobs whilst in the sixth form without success and was concerned about the sort of future work she could secure, even with the help of a degree.

Following a similar line of argument to Holly, Georgia (white British, working class) also felt that getting a job after gaining a degree was also problematic and precarious:

And you are working for the rest of your life after university... But in reality sometimes it's hard to get a job after you get your degree, so you are not sure if you actually will get a job at the end of it... and it costs a lot of money.

Georgia's view highlights a sense of precarity associated with undertaking a degree and finding herself unable to locate suitable, graduate employment. The concerns expressed by Holly and Georgia are not unfounded as a glance at the graduate employment rates for 2015 reveal that 87.1% of graduates and 87.9% of post-graduates were employed compared with 69.7% non-graduates (Department for Business, Innovation and Skills (DfBIS) 2015). However, further analysis of these figures reveals a more complex picture:

> although graduates and postgraduates had similar overall employment rates in 2015 (around 87%), postgraduates had much greater high skilled employment rates, with 78% of all working age postgraduates in high skill employment compared to 66% of all working age graduates. The young population had lower high skilled employment rates than the overall working age population across all qualification categories, perhaps suggesting it might take time for young people to become established in the labour market or to reach the higher levels in organisations that are captured by the high skilled employment rate measure. (DfBIS 2015: 9)

The DfBIS data show some significant differences in the employment prospects available to graduates when compared with non-graduates. Younger people require more time to climb the labour market ladder, regardless of their qualifications. The increase in zero hours contracts and the growth in service sector jobs has contributed to a diversified labour market where there are greater numbers of semi-skilled and unskilled forms of labour compared with the availability of high skilled work (DfBIS 2015).

Sian (white British, working class) also talked about the possibility of applying for a job, but like Holly, she was not sure what sort of job she would be able to find. But Sian attributed her own lack of certainty to her own indecision about not knowing what she wanted to do in the future. She talked about friends who had obtained apprenticeships and were earning more than friends who had obtained graduate qualifications:

> Fair enough people say that if you go to uni you'll get like a higher job, higher opportunities, but if you don't go to uni you could work your way up in the same amount of years. I know some people that have done

apprenticeships and stuff, and they are earning like so much, compared to people that come out and can't even find a job.

The 'earn while you learn' aspect of apprenticeships was appealing to those participants not certain about their future study or employment plans. Sian explained that she was not sure what she was interested in and she was going to wait for her results and 'take it from there'. This 'wait and see' sentiment was echoed in Holly, Stephanie and Georgia's discussions for the future.

When discussing her plans for the future, Stephanie (white British, middle class) was very unsure about what to do for her next steps and the worry of debt was pushing her towards considering work:

> *Steph:* I still don't know. I haven't a clue . . . I don't know until I get my results what I'm going to do, I'll wait and see. I just don't know about uni . . .
>
> *KH:* Why would uni be off-putting?
>
> *Steph:* It's like whether I want to study again for another three years, and mainly because it's really expensive. I wouldn't want to go and be getting into debt when I could be earning money, I think. So that's why I'm thinking of looking for a job.

Stephanie's ambivalence towards higher education is reflected in her concerns about taking on high levels of debt versus obtaining paid employment. Stephanie went on to cite the example of a friend who had found employment after leaving school and was now earning a respectable salary. Despite Stephanie's middle-class family background, she was reluctant to take on the debt associated with gaining graduate status.

Sian, Holly, Stephanie and Georgia seemed reluctant to offer any certainty in their potential future choices and were very unsure about whether university would be worthwhile for them. Their ambivalence highlights the fluid nature of the employment market at the time of the focus groups alongside the pressure created by university tuition fees. Brown and Lauder (2013) have noted the competition created by the global auction that has pushed governments around the world to compete for skilled jobs. The authors argue that 'while the global labour market may narrow some aspects of global inequalities, it has contributed to widening domestic inequalities' in relation to job opportunities (Brown and Lauder 2013: 20). The inequalities they refer to relate to those who can access the opportunities to study and gain the qualifications necessary to compete in the global context:

> For a lucky few, often from very privileged backgrounds, the global auction will remain in forward gear as their investments of effort, time, and money will be handsomely rewarded. But most others, including those with a college education, will struggle to achieve the trappings of a middle-class lifestyle, with shrinking pay checks, longer working hours, inferior retirement provision, reduced health care coverage, declining career prospects, and greater job insecurity. In this cut-price competition of brainpower, workers will be forced to do more for less. (Brown and Lauder 2013: 20)

The LEO (2016) data reinforces the issue of whether earning versus learning is best for young people's future, highlighting the relatively low salaries achieved by several graduates. A further issue relates to the area of study, which will have a significant impact on potential future earnings as argued by Walker and Zhu (2011). Graduate jobs are arguably often referred to as a homogenous group, but in reality, there are myriad different forms of graduate work – some are highly skilled and professional, some are administrative and semi-skilled. This disparity between the status and potential earnings available to graduates depending on their field of study contributes towards significant inequalities within the graduate group.

Jamal (Pakistani, unsure of class background) talked about the issue and difficulty he perceived he would face when distinguishing himself from other students given that many young people would be going after similar qualifications and similar degrees. I raised the possibility of working up through a company, a theme that had been discussed earlier in the focus group, and Jamal discussed his views about this possible pathway to employment:

> *KH:*   What about the working-your-way-up idea you mentioned? Doesn't that appeal?
>
> *Jamal:*   It does, but I think, like, you need a degree to get anywhere, because everyone's gonna have it, but you've got to compete with other people. So maybe it would be better to have the experience actually, because that's what everyone's looking for, for example I've applied for about fifty jobs, and for all of them it's like...well personally I think I haven't got it, because I haven't

got experience, I haven't worked anywhere else, and I see people who already have a job getting like three or four other jobs as well because they've had that experience, so it's easier, and jobs just come to them easily. But at the same time I think the whole experience of actually being in university, and like all the surroundings and everything, is probably better than being just out in the world of work and stuff.

Jamal highlights the dilemma of studying versus attempting to gain employment. He explained his own experience of applying for over 50 jobs with no success as a consequence of his lack of experience. He perceived that the difficulty of getting a foot into the employment door, compounded by a lack of qualifications, created a dilemma for young people as they progress from school to university or work. Those students in the sample who worked, even in low-paid and low-skilled jobs, were perhaps at an advantage when compared with their peers who did not possess work experience. The difficulties in ensuring clear and successful pathways to employment are reflected in recent institutional drives to increase 'work-integrated learning (WIL) as part of a university education are framed within the agenda to enhance graduate employability' (Tran and Soejatminah 2016: 1). Relatedly, Walsh (2015) has claimed that many disadvantaged young people seeking employment are frequently forced out of considering higher education and pushed towards 'low level training courses' because of the lack of viable employment alternatives.

These examples highlight the ambivalent perspectives held by a minority of the young people in the sample towards employment versus university for their future plans. The increase in tuition fees was a key factor in their reluctance to apply for university. But they were also aware of the need for work experience to gain employment and they were concerned about the value of a degree if they did not have the relevant work experience to support their applications. Sian (white British, working class) cited the example of friends on apprenticeship programmes who were earning more than their graduate peers because of the 'earn while you learn' philosophy underpinning apprenticeships. The participants' responses here were also linked to the need to have more than just qualifications and work experience. Their discussions highlighted the need to build social capital whilst studying to enable them to compete in the employment market.

ACCESSING EMPLOYMENT: BONDING AND BRIDGING SOCIAL CAPITAL

Two of the participants talked about the importance of family and community networks in assisting access to non-graduate employment. Both participants identified the importance of who you know, rather than what you know:

> I think it's that, if you know people, I've got two jobs and I've got them both because I know people in them. So it's not really what you know. (Holly, white British, unsure of class background/probably middle class)

> As I said earlier, I think it's more based on who you know. If you or your family know people who can get you into a good job then you can go a long way. (Paresh, Indian, middle class)

The usefulness and value of social networks does depend on the social class and social advantage of the individual seeking to deploy the available resources. As Putnam (2001: 321) points out:

> Not only do residents of extreme poverty areas have fewer social ties but they also tend to have ties of less social worth, as measured by the social position of their partners, parents, siblings and best friends, for instance. In short they possess lower volumes of social capital.

Paresh is from a middle-class background and Holly identified herself as 'probably' from a middleclass background, suggesting that both students on the basis of their social class background have access to more valuable social networks and possess valued forms of social capital. The possession of valuable forms of social capital has the potential to convert into access to valuable social networks, which in turn can provide access to greater opportunities.

NARROWING OF POST-18 OPTIONS: THE TEACHERS' PERCEPTIONS OF NON-GRADUATE EMPLOYMENT POSSIBILITIES AND PATHWAYS

Similarly to the students, the teachers expressed concern about the limited post-18 pathways available to those young people not intending to study either at university or as part of a vocationally orientated course. The shrinking youth employment market has been of increasing concern to educators and parents over the past two decades, due to recession and credentialisation of the employment market (Gunderson and Fazio 2014; Archer et al. 2010). The changing employment structures that have emerged since widespread de-industrialisation within England has significantly reduced youth employment opportunities for those from working-class backgrounds (Archer et al. 2010). The pathways to semi-skilled, working-class employment identified by Willis (1977) in the 1960s and early 1970s, such as manufacturing, have almost disappeared, leaving a yet to be filled gap in the employment market. The recent increase in service jobs, from working in telesales to working as a barrister, are increasingly becoming graduate jobs as recent decades of grade inflation and credentialisation begin to exert an impact on youth employment. As Moore (2012: 117) points out:

> The reduction in educational inequality at given levels is associated with credential inflation in the labour market so that everyone simply needs more education in order to stay in the same place.

Clearly, the working classes are not the only group affected by high levels of youth unemployment. Young people from middle-class families are also experiencing pressure when it comes to securing youth employment (Hoskins and Barker 2014; Barker and Hoskins 2015), particularly those without graduate level qualifications. Recent figures from the ONS reveal that young people across the class spectrum are disproportionately represented in unemployment figures:

> Young people are nearly three times more likely to be unemployed than the rest of the population, the largest gap in more than 20 years, according to an analysis of official figures. The number of people aged 16–24 who are not in full-time education or employment has increased by 8,000 over the last quarter. With 498,000 in that age group without a job, an analysis by the House of Commons library for Labour shows that young people now fare comparatively worse than at any point since 1992. Their unemployment rate is 14.4%. The overall unemployment rate now stands at 5.7% of the total working population, according to the Office for National Statistics (ONS) (Boffey 2015).

The data confirm that those young people deciding not to pursue university qualifications due to the soaring costs associated with higher education are finding their alternative options are significantly limited.

OFSTED rated good and outstanding schools are focussed on higher education to the exclusion of alternative post-18 pathways (Hoskins and Barker 2014). The intensive focus on higher education at Parkfield contributed to the young people in the study feeling that they were being squeezed into ever-narrower pathways.

The teachers were very aware of this pressure to participate in higher education and all expressed dismay about the consequence of the school's emphasis on university participation, which they perceived to be at the exclusion of other possible post-18 pathways. Several of the teachers identified the lack of viable alternative pathways as a reductive way of working with young people who had a lot to give back to their communities and wider society, but who were not academically orientated. A related issue that arose from the focus on higher education was the lack of work experience, which Jamal (Pakistani, unsure of class background) had similarly identified as a barrier to progression. For example, Emily (Head of Post 16 Study Sociology, white British) was aware of the tension between gaining qualifications and gaining employment, highlighting that in her view, many employers look for evidence of experience alongside qualifications as opposed to qualifications alone:

In the current economic climate people can't get graduate jobs, the jobs that they are getting, you know, the people who are getting the jobs are people who are already in the industry, working their way up, and there are so many people coming out with degrees now that people consider how can you tell between one and another? We were saying this to our girls...you know, do work experience, if you can get good references, if you've gone in and you've done work experience, that will be a foot in the door, and sometimes you have to go in at the bottom. And that's the other thing, people are thinking.... You know you hear all these stories about people going in at the bottom, and think if I carry on for another three years I've got this thirty thousand, and if I am going to start with everybody else at the bottom what was the point of it?

The pressure to 'get a foot in the door' has contributed to the growth of unpaid internships, which provide a 'valuable way of gaining initial access to an institution and achieving experience in a professional sphere' (Roberts and Evans 2013: 85). These authors note that young people from middle-class families, who have the right sorts of networks and family connections, are more likely than those from working-class families to gain access to internships (Roberts and Evans 2013). Those young people from working-class families are instead directed towards work experience, which has been criticised for 'pushing young unemployed people into unpaid short term positions (largely in unskilled work) for large corporations' (Roberts and Evans 2013: 85). The limited possession of valued forms of social capital available to many working-class families has consequences for the sorts of employment opportunities they can access to aid and assist their children. Whilst those working- and middle-class young people rejecting higher education in pursuit of employment face challenges in their attempts to access employment, through unpaid internships, the middle classes are better positioned to access professional employment through their family networks, thus ensuring social reproduction from one generation to the next.

Maria (White British, Year 12/Post 16 Teacher) echoed Emily's views about the importance of gaining relevant experience as well as qualifications as the key to obtaining employment:

> Recently employers have come out and praised vocational qualifications, BTEC business studies, and the childcare course, you know, when you send your child into, I think it was in the news recently, why would a nursery nurse or somebody working in childcare need to have any qualifications? Well, I think as a parent, you know, if you've got two people applying for a job and you've got one who's studied childcare for two years for a vocational qualification, and one who hasn't, and has just got their GCSEs, well surely you are going to go for the student who's got experience working in child-care for two years. And it just seems that employers are saying – we like this – but the government don't want it, because I don't think it fits into their agenda of what they want education to be.

Maria raises interesting points about the mismatch between the sorts of skills and levels of experience that employers want from potential employees, compared with what the government would like young people to do. Perhaps the pressure created by youth unemployment in the United Kingdom, which has resulted in the government increasing the school leaving age to 18, is not helpful to employers seeking employees with experience. The credentialisation that has been taking place in education for several decades requires young people to gain more qualifications for semi-skilled forms of work (Halsey et al. 1980). The move towards vocational education has opened up opportunities for young people from working-class backgrounds, but these opportunities are now in decline due to a change in policy direction by the government.

Maria's views about the importance of work experience are supported by research carried out by Searle et al. (2014), who found that:

> According to National Association of Colleges and Employers' survey (2014), three out of four recruiters state that they prefer job candidates with relevant experience. Work experience is found to be a good predictor of later quality and stability of employment for young people. (Ling and O'Brien 2012) (cited in Searle et al. 2014)

In my sample several of the young people had made similar points such as Jamal (Pakistani, unsure of class background) who had applied for over 50 jobs but did not get short-listed for any interviews, which he attributed to his lack of experience.

John (White British, Head of Post 16 Study), Chole (White British, Year 12/Post 16 Teacher) and Daniel (White British, Year 12/Post 16 Teacher) were also concerned about the emphasis on graduate post-18 pathways to the exclusion of alternative from of provision:

> We do need people doing some other non-graduate jobs, we can't have everyone demanding, you know, and employers are saying because all the graduates are coming out wanting jobs, no one wants to do the other jobs anymore, even though they can be as good, and can lead to good earning potential, they are not doing that, so everyone's coming out thinking I am a graduate, therefore I must earn thirty thousand pounds a year, or twenty-five, whatever it is they are unrealistically expecting now. But what about all the people that can start down and move up? (John, Head of Post 16 Study)

> I don't think we should be putting the masses that we are putting to uni through uni, so they can come out and be working on sixteen thousand pounds a year when they could have done that straight from their A levels or something. I think this problem is being looked at backwards. (Chole, White British, Year 12/Post 16 Teacher)

> *Daniel:*   But also I think that if the government is doing that they need to really think about how the schools provide a route for students to go on to get jobs... which is very important, because a lot of the students who do the vocational courses don't want to go to university, but then sometimes the advice and provision for

them isn't particularly good. We've got advisors in the school, but as teachers, I mean I used to work in industry, but I've kind of lost touch now, because I've been out for a long time, what kind of advice do we give them, and how are these employers coming into school, and surely there should be a much better link between employment and schools.

KH: What sort of employers are you thinking of?

Daniel: A cross-section. We are in London, why aren't businesses linked to schools? We are in a big pool, why isn't the government pushing it so there's a direct route from schools to employment?

The shortage of youth post-18 employment possibilities requires schools to take a broader look at their post-18 pathways and provision and to consider how best to support those students not pursuing academic courses. But for any initiatives to be viable, they require the support of government through policy legislation.

The data here and in Chapter 4 suggests the need for a broader careers guidance provision within Parkfield School. The school's focus on academic pathways excludes those young people seeking vocational or employment opportunities at the age of 18. Several of the student and staff participants noted that there is extremely limited help and assistance available to young people following non-academic pathways. Daniel (White British, Year 12/Post 16 Teacher) highlights the need for partnerships between Parkfield School and businesses to boost the potential employment prospects for his students.

APPRENTICESHIPS

One of the preferred alternative pathways to higher education is that of apprenticeships. Once a promising pathway into skilled and semi-skilled employment for working-class young people, apprenticeships have retracted substantially in recent decades (Ainley and Allen 2010). The reasons for the demise of apprenticeships include a lack of employers willing to participate in apprenticeship schemes, a growing perception on the part of parents and students that a degree is needed for almost all forms of employment and the long standing association that apprenticeships share with blue-collar forms of employment (Wright 2015).

The teachers at Parkfield were positive about the potential opportunities created by apprenticeships. However, as exemplified by Daniel, the teachers identified that the challenge facing students was accessing these opportunities:

> There are apprenticeships out there, but again it's well, where are they, how do I find them, what do I need to do to get on it? The advice that we've had is pretty much non-existent from what I understand. (Daniel, White British, Year 12/Post 16 Teacher)

The students similarly highlighted the difficulty of accessing information about apprenticeships through the school support structures. The emphasis on higher education participation at Parkfield School minimised the time and space dedicated to providing information about alternative pathways.

Julia (White Irish, Year 12/Post 16 Teacher) commented that the support available to those students seeking to pursue an apprenticeship had decreased in recent years:

> In previous years when we used to have more apprenticeships and that was really good because the kids, I can actually think of one or two students that I have who are like little caged animals, you know they want to get out and work and they can't do it, so they have to sit in this kind of caged environment, and it's just really bad for them, whereas if they'd started an apprenticeship and started to learn something they'd be out working, doing things.

Julia highlights the reduction in access to apprenticeships and the associated implications for some of her students who needed the opportunity to earn and learn. According to a recent report by City and Guilds (2016: 2) noted that the profile of Vocational Education and Training (VET) has dramatically increased, driven mainly by the needs of businesses, and yet the authors point out that:

> Britain is still battling the stigma that university is the best route to employment. In 1999, former Prime Minister Tony Blair announced his plans for 50% of young people to go to university. This, coupled with schools being measured on how many students attend university, has led to young people being pushed to pursue academia.

These apprenticeship access challenges facing the teachers at Parkfield School highlight the need for alternative pathways to the academic routes pursued by many of their students. The concerns raised by Julia and Daniel highlight the missed opportunities at the school level to ensure all students can maximise their future potential, regardless of their academic ability.

CONCLUDING REMARKS: THE NEED FOR AN ALTERNATIVE VISION OF EDUCATION

The key aim of this chapter has been to explore the alternative pathways available to those students not intending to pursue higher education. The data highlights the concerns of the teachers and students at Parkfield School in relation to the lack of alternative provision and support for non-graduate pathways in a graduate dominated world. The students were concerned about the school's relentless emphasis that they should be applying for university, regardless of their suitability to attend or their desire to participate in higher education.

The increases in youth unemployment suggest that leaving school at the age of 18 years to find a job is a risky business. The prevalence of zero hours contracts and the casualisation of work have resulted in a generation of young people facing limited opportunities and prospects. The credentialisation of employment also impacts on the forms of work available to young people. The need to gain ever more credentials for semi-skilled forms of work has reduced the range of possible employment available to young people leaving school with limited qualifications and limited work experience (Moore 2012). The need to gain work experience was identified by participants as a key factor in unlocking the employment market. For example, Jamal had applied for in excess of 50 jobs and had not managed to secure a single offer. Several of the teachers had noted that employers preferred to give employment to those young people who had some form of work experience, but getting a foot in the door to obtain such experience was not easy. Those young people in the sample such as Holly, who had managed to gain employment, had done so through social networks, highlighting the value of social capital in accessing limited opportunities in the current context.

The teachers highlighted the need for greater investment in VET and apprenticeships as a way of equalising opportunities for young people. The unequal weighting given to academic pathways when compared with vocational routes to employment needs to be addressed. The teachers emphasised that the current system in England of post-16 and post-18 education favours university education over other pathways to employment, particularly apprenticeships. Yet these vocational opportunities can provide a meaningful and fulfilling experience for young people from a range of backgrounds who are not academically orientated.

Set against the current context where the emphasis is on 'graduation, graduation, graduation', the data suggest that there is a need for an alternative model for post-18 opportunities that provides greater access to vocationally orientated routes to work and a greater number of such routes to work. But it is crucial that vocational pathways are not perceived as inferior in status and opportunity to that of a graduate pathway. The need for more post-18 pathways to work is perhaps one of the most pressing challenges facing the government if they are to meet the task of providing employment for all, regardless of social identity, including social class, gender and ethnicity. A new vision for youth education and employment is required to ensure that no young person is left behind, or excluded from fulfilling their potential on the basis of their academic performance.

CHAPTER 6

The Contemporary Context of Youth Participation and Identities: Challenging the Status Quo

INTRODUCTION

During her speech setting out her vision for the future of the state education system in England the recently appointed Conservative Prime Minister, Theresa May (2016-ongoing), stated that her key aim is to achieve a fair and meritocratic system:

> I want Britain to be a place where advantage is based on merit not privilege; where it's your talent and hard work that matter, not where you were born, who your parents are or what your accent sounds like. (Lillicot 2016)

Such a vision is commendable. However, successive prime ministers and their government ministers have espoused their desire to help all young people, regardless of their background, to achieve their potential through what they perceive to be an inclusive education system that does not simply reproduce advantage and disadvantage. However, in practice, through policy changes including the Conservative's removal of EMA and the increase in university tuition fees, the policy reality and outcomes for young people have been at variance with their and May's aims. Despite politicians' stated desire to equalise the education playing field, the further and higher education policy reality remains rooted in social division, social immobility and social reproduction.

© The Author(s) 2017
K. Hoskins, *Youth Identities, Education and Employment,*
Policy and Practice in the Classroom,
DOI 10.1057/978-1-137-35292-7_6

Throughout this book I have examined how young people's gender, social class and ethnic identity continue to influence what is and what is not possible as they leave compulsory education, despite discourses of meritocracy circulated and maintained by the government, senior school leaders and teachers. A related aim has been to examine the role of policy in enabling and constraining young people's horizons for the future. In addition, I have explored the plans and imagined futures of those young people seeking to move on from education and secure non-graduate employment, reflecting on their teachers' views and perceptions about the challenges facing these students. Comparisons have been made to the youth employment and higher education contexts in Greece and Spain to consider differences and similarities between these two countries' contexts and the impact of this on young people. In what follows, I review the key findings in light of the research questions and highlight the key issues arising from the data.

Post-16 and Post-18 Pathways – The Enduring Influence of Identity

The research sought to understand if and how the participants' identity influenced their post-16 and post-18 decisions. The findings from the project confirm that identity continues to exert a defining influence on the intended pathways of young people. All the participants in my sample "'knew their limits" in relation to post-compulsory educational routes' (Archer and Yamashita 2003: 53). The data has demonstrated that the social class of the family a child is born into, alongside their gender and ethnicity, are decisive ingredients that shape and influence future pathways, trajectories and aspirations. There is determinism embedded in this claim; however, the literature review in Chapter 2 and data analysis reveals that the effectiveness of individual agency, no matter how ambitious an individual's aspirations are, is still challenged and limited by social structures and stereotypes, which continue to create and perpetuate social injustice.

A good example of social injustice was evident in the participants' discussions about the removal of EMA. The students from working-class families who would have qualified to receive EMA needed to make up the lost funds through working long hours in low paid, insecure and low status work. Not surprisingly, the impact of this employment pressure on the participants resulted in less time to dedicate to their studies, less time to work on their university applications, no leisure time and tiredness from working long shifts. However, many of the students who would not have qualified to receive the funds perceived the removal of EMA as fair and just and showed little empathy for their less economically fortunate peers. The lack of understanding displayed by the students towards their peers evidences Giddens' (Giddens 1991) assertion that some young people are highly individualised and preoccupied with their own success with limited regard for less fortunate others.

The analysis in Chapters 3, 4 and 5 revealed that gender, social class and ethnicity impact on the choices that young people make about their educational pathway and future employment. Subject choices at post-16 were stratified according to gender with girls more likely to select arts and humanities subjects and boys more likely to select science, mathematics and business studies – although the participants repeatedly rejected any suggestion that their choices related to their gender. For example, the boys were intending to pursue higher status careers, that is, Tim (white British, middle class) planned to work in biomedicine and Jamal (Pakistani, unsure of class background) in economics. There was evidence of girls seeking a somewhat diverse range of career pathways, for example, Adele's (Black African-Caribbean, middle class) desire to become a doctor. However, several of the girls held gendered aspirations for careers in teaching and social work.

Ethnicity had impacted on those students from minority ethnic backgrounds including Adele (Black African-Caribbean, middle class) and Ann (Black African-Caribbean, working class) who both perceived that they needed to 'work harder' than their white British peers to prove their worth because 'for some ethnic groups it's so much easier to break into some areas of work', such as medicine. Paresh (Indian, middle class) was aware of the stereotypes associated with her Indian ethnic identity around being academically capable, which is often due to parental pressure to succeed academically, something Paresh had not directly experienced. Those students from white British backgrounds did not experience their ethnicity as a prohibitive factor in shaping their future trajectories and whiteness is unproblematically experienced as the norm at Parkfield School. This finding suggests that Parkfield School like many other British secondary schools (Mirza 2009; Rollock et al. 2014) has more work to do to raise awareness amongst the students of the impact of ethnicity on black and minority ethnic students (BME) in terms of their choices and opportunities within the education system.

Social class background influenced the participant's aspirations for their imagined futures and their plans for their post-16 and post-18 pathways were overwhelmingly rooted in their family habitus. The students reported on the influence of parents and extended family in directing and guiding their future plans. Several of the students from middle-class families aspired to attend Russell Group universities and study high status subjects. Those participants from working-class families tended to aspire to more vocational higher education pathways or intended to seek employment or an apprenticeship scheme at the age of 18 years. The students were not aware of the influence of social class on their pathways and attributed their future plans to their own agency and choices.

The influence of social class, gender and ethnicity was important in shaping the majority of the participant's imagined futures, and yet not acknowledged by most of them. There were some exceptions to this pattern, notably Adele (Black African-Caribbean, middle class) and Ann (Black African-Caribbean, working class) who acknowledged how their ethnicity had influenced them, and Jodie (white British, working class) and Laura (White British, middle class) were aware that their gender had shaped their subject choices and career aspirations. Social class was the most elusive influence for the participants to acknowledge and only Kim (Chinese, working class) briefly reflected on the ways in which social class and associated financial struggles could impact on the further and higher educational choice-making processes.

The enduring influence of identity on choices and experiences highlights the need for parents, schools and teachers to continue challenging stereotypes to ensure that all young people, regardless of their background, are provided with the practical tools and advice to fulfil their ambitions for the future. A key area for improvement identified by staff and students at Parkfield School related to the careers advice available to students. The staff and students perceived that this advice was too focused on higher education to the exclusion of alternative pathways, particularly apprenticeships. The government's recent commitment to apprenticeships has been articulated through the 'English Apprenticeships: Our 2020 Vision' (HM Government 2016). The goal of this initiative is

> for young people to see apprenticeships as a high quality and prestigious path to successful careers, and for these opportunities to be available across all sectors of the economy, in all parts of the country and at all levels. (HM Government 2016: 2)

The teachers and several of the students at Parkfield School would support the need for this form of intervention in post-18 provision. To ensure parity between apprenticeships and higher education, employers need to take a central role in ensuring equality in their recruitment processes and job specification requirements.

But apprenticeships are not the only area that requires attention in terms of creating employability parity between different forms of qualifications. A key finding of the analysis relates to the differentiated value associated with different degree subject areas and courses of study. The teachers and students were aware that not all degrees have the same economic exchange value in the employment market. For example, those students in the sample seeking a graduate career in social care and childcare such as Susie (White British, middle class) and Gemma (White British, middle class) expected to earn significantly less over the duration of their working lives than Adele (Black African-Caribbean, middle class) who intends to pursue a career in medicine and Tim (White British, middle class) who plans to work as a biochemist. The uneven distribution of wages across differentiated graduate employment pathways raises important questions about the value of degrees in particular fields. For example, the social sciences, arts and humanities which tend to lead to less well-remunerated jobs than the sciences. This contributes to an unequal hierarchy within graduate and postgraduate education and employment. The research findings suggest that to provide greater equity higher education tuition fees need to account for the future employability of students and the associated costs for programmes of study.

Additionally, the teachers discussed at length the importance of the institutional value of a degree and actively encouraged all their students to apply for a place at a Russell Group institution where possible. Parkfield School benefits from this selective approach to higher education destinations in terms of the potential to reproduce the school's middle-class cohort. However, this pressure to encourage students to apply to Russell Group institutions resulted in some participants and most of the teachers acknowledging the marginalisation experienced by some of the less academically capable students. There was general agreement in the focus groups and interviews that the emphasis at Parkfield School on applying for a place at an elite institution was detrimental to those students planning to attend a post-1992 institution and particularly for those intending to leave school at the age of 18 years and seek either an apprenticeship or employment. All of the teachers were reflexive about the pressure to graduate and noted the limitations this placed on many students who would be better suited to employment.

The emphasis on Russell Group participation had resulted in many of the teachers identifying the need for more vocational higher education pathways to accommodate the needs of students who have a great deal to offer potential employers. For example, Daniel told me that:

> If you think about university courses, there already are university courses that are generally vocational, there's a large element of coursework, a large element of independent work. Whereas the traditional GCSEs, I mean let's face it, kids get coached to do their GCSEs. Yes, our teaching has improved massively, our understanding about teaching has improved, and students have got better information...But I think the government forgets that university courses still have that element of vocational study, if there's coursework in there, it's not all exams. So I wonder if they've thought about that. (Daniel, Year 12/Post 16 Teacher)

Referring to Michel Gove's (former Secretary of State for Education 2010–2014) attempts to increase academic excellence in schools (Gove 2011a, 2011b), Daniel was particularly concerned by the proposed reductions to vocational pathways available at post-16 and post-18 and the lack of government consultation in terms of these changes. He explained that:

> We spent a long time in the school raising the profile of vocational studies, to a point where we were getting students excellent grades, parents were really aware of the value of vocational studies, we were also able to teach students in a different way, that suited their learning needs, so they were able to progress and get good qualifications. And I think that the way the government is changing it, without consultation, without thinking about the processes, is destroying the value that it brings.

Daniel's perspective on the impact of the changes to vocational education provision at post-16 and post-18 was reflected across the sample of teachers who all felt that vocational as well as academic educational pathways needed to be protected in the interests of social justice and improved outcomes for all pupils. All the teachers interviewed argued that the government should increase vocational post-18 degree pathways to broaden access to higher education to all students. In so doing, students from a wide range of backgrounds could be provided with the opportunity to engage in a form of higher education, in an increasingly graduate orientated world.

Turning briefly to the European higher education context, the findings in the book are highly relevant to the Spanish and Greek education systems as they face increasing pressure to review the costs of providing higher education against the backdrop of extended austerity over a prolonged period. An important consideration emerging from this research is the way Spanish and Greek governments structure any future higher education tuition fee increases. The data analysis presented here suggests that the field of study and potential future earnings should be an important consideration for any newly introduced higher education tuition fee structure. Whilst differentiating between fields of study could be incredibly problematic for HEIs and academic staff, from the students' and their parents' perspectives such changes could ensure a fairer fee system that directly relates to future earning capacity. To further support the participation of students in higher education, these countries could also consider post-16 financial support to the most disadvantaged students to enable their continued participation in education and to provide a pathway for students to access university.

Additionally, the status of higher education, vocational education and employment pathways would also benefit from equalised status. Spain and Greece have experienced considerable pressure in relation to the manufacturing sector (Zmas 2014) and the shrinking manufacturing base in both countries has impacted on the recent economic turbulence in both countries (Williams-Grut 2015). By broadening out vocational higher education these countries could enable participation of greater numbers of students in university education.

POST-16 AND POST-18 PATHWAYS – THE ROLE OF PARENTS AND TEACHERS

Chapters 3, 4 and 5 highlighted the important support that the students received from their teachers and that many received from their parents. The teachers were particularly supportive towards those students applying for higher education. Students reported assistance from their teachers with writing their UCAS applications, providing advice about their intended programme of study and providing advice about the institution they should apply to. The teachers arranged higher education talks to maximise student's university applications. The level of institutional support for those students considering higher education was highlighted numerous times in the interviews and focus groups.

The teachers were also committed to supporting students with vocational pathways at post-16, but this support was not available at the post-18 transition. For example, those students who might have benefitted from an apprenticeship at the age of 18 found themselves left to navigate the options without institutional support. Georgia is a good example of a student who felt unsupported in her post-18 choices by her teachers. She was keen to investigate alternative pathways upon leaving school at 18, but she told me that the teachers 'briefly mentioned apprenticeships and work, but it's mainly focused on the universities, so I find it harder to work out what I want to do'. The teachers focus on higher education was to the detriment of those students who sought alternative provision.

The students reported receiving a lot of support from their parents or extended family. Without exception, students had experienced advice from a family member about their post-16 and post-18 pathways. The advice received was relational to the student's social class background. For example, those students intending to apply to a Russell Group university, such as Beth, Claudia and Tim, had all received parental support and encouragement to pursue this goal. Their parents had attended elite universities and this insider knowledge, alongside the support received from the school, resulted in some students finding themselves in an advantaged position when compared to their less privileged peers. Those students whose parents had not attended university, such as Sian, did not push their children towards higher education. Thus, in support of other research (Hoskins and Barker 2014; Reay et al. 2013, 2010) examples of social reproduction arising from the family milieu were apparent in the case study. Family support along with teacher support were key in assisting those students intending to apply to university with that process. However, there were disruptions to this pattern of family support aimed at achieving social reproduction as evident in the stories of Holly and Stephanie who are from middle-class families where university participation is the norm, but who are not intending to apply due to the higher education tuition fee costs.

YOUTH UN/EMPLOYMENT

Chapter 5 addresses research question three and explores how the participants' plans are shaped by the current employment context. The chapter confirms that very few of the participants are considering leaving school at

18 to seek employment. Sian, Georgia (both white British, working class), Holly (white British, unsure of class background/probably middle class) and Stephanie (white British, middle class) are considering seeking employment because they were put off higher education participation due to the increase higher education tuition fees. They cited examples of friends who had worked their way up through companies to achieve status and a good salary and argued that taking on debt did not make financial sense to them. Despite the high rates of youth unemployment, all these students felt that finding work was preferable to higher education participation. Whilst the wider employment context was a concern for these young people, they had decided to pursue employment in the hope that they too could work their way up through the ranks and secure professional occupations through gaining on the job experience. The data suggests that those young people considering employment were less concerned about the impact of recession on their potential to gain a job than they were about the impact of taking on high levels of student debt on their future lives.

THE POTENTIAL OF A MULTI-DIMENSIONAL SOCIAL JUSTICE APPROACH TO EQUALISE YOUTH OPPORTUNITIES

The findings from the research highlight the need for social justice interventions into the provision of and access to post-16 and post-18 educational opportunities and improved youth employment prospects for those students ready to leave education. The analysis reveals that white, male and female students from privileged class backgrounds are more likely to aspire to and access elite universities and elite programmes of study than their working-class, minority ethnic peers. To equalise access to post-16 and post-18 study in England, social justice interventions need to go beyond simplistic notions of a singular approach, that is, distributional, relational or associational (Fraser 1997). Distributional social justice 'refers to the principles by which goods are distributed in society' (Gewirtz 1998: 470). Relational social justice refers to 'the nature of the relationships which structure society' (Gewirtz 1998: 471). Associational social justice can be viewed as 'both an end in itself and a means to the ends of economic and cultural justice' (Gewirtz and Cribb 2002: 503).

To apply plural social justice considerations to further and higher educational opportunities there needs to be acknowledgement that 'opportunity...is a condition of enablement' (Young 1990: 26). Therefore, as

Gewirtz (1998: 142) argues, we only 'have opportunities if we are not constrained from doing things'. In other words:

> The extent to which we have opportunities depends upon the enabling possibilities generated by the rules and practices of the society within which we operate, and by the ways in which people treat each other in that society. (Gewirtz 1998: 142)

Gewirtz (1998) argues that society needs to provide a multi-dimensional approach to social justice, which includes the distributional, relational and associational forms of justice. As such, when 'evaluating social justice according to whether persons have opportunities' we must, according to Young (1990: 26) evaluate 'not a distributive outcome but the social structures that enable or constrain the individuals in relevant situations'. Variants such as gender, social class and ethnicity all come to bear on these situations, shaping aspirations, expectations and access to opportunities. In an unequal society, where the dominant social group – that is white and middle/upper class – maintains the status quo, we need plural conceptualisations of social justice to enable more equal access and outcomes for all social groups regardless of their identity.

The data analysis throughout this book points to the need for a more socially just education system that disrupts well-established patterns of social reproduction. Those students from middle-class families had the aspirations, guidance and resources to access reified social goods. For example, all the students planning to apply to a Russell Group institution had a middle-class family habitus. Upon entering the school, these students were then further supported by their teachers who assisted their plans in pragmatic ways – for example, by providing help with their university applications. Parkside School's habitus was circumscribed by a middle-class ethos and the teachers aimed to maximise university attendance amongst their student cohort. These aims are not necessarily problematic, but the reality for those students not planning on applying to university was a sense of marginalisation.

The data provided powerful stories that reveal how keenly those students intending to apply to university along with their teachers seem to feel the pressures to achieve – for themselves and for their school. The student and teacher stories revealed the extent to which they needed to be academically successful for their future and for the reputation of the school. The students planning to leave school at 18 and seek employment received very minimal practical help and support with, for example, writing a cover letter or curriculum vitae. They reported the non-existent careers advice they had received and a sense that they were overlooked by their teachers. A plural conception of social justice could enable educators to engage with all the students, regardless of their intended post-16 and post-18 pathway. The emphasis on academic attainment at Parkside School, similarly to many other schools within England (Maguire et al. 2011), has resulted in a narrowly focussed education system that prioritises supporting academically capable students and marginalises vocationally or employment orientated students.

The findings highlight the potential benefits that could arise from the reintroduction of post-16 financial support in the form of EMA or a comparable allowance for those students who would have benefitted from the funds. There is also a need to revisit higher education tuition fee structures, particularly in terms of the very different earning capacity of graduates entering the employment market, depending on their field of study. The participants have different aspirations about the university they hope to attend, the programme of study they intend to pursue and the resultant graduate employment they seek to achieve; yet they will all pay approximately the same in tuition fees.

The data analysis confirms that the recent changes in post-16 and post-18 education policy context serve to reinforce the privilege and opportunity of already privileged students. The findings highlight the need for social justice interventions in education to level the social and economic playing field between students, and to challenge the gender and ethnic stereotypes that persist in shaping young people's aspirations for their imagined futures. The analysis also indicates that a reconceptualisation of vocational education is required in order to equalise the status between academic and vocational pathways available to young people. The emphasis on narrow, academic skills is of limited use to employers and will not meet the needs of England's economy.

To sum up, it remains the case at Parkfield School that educational differences are indeed frequently misrecognised as resulting from individual giftedness rather than from classed, gendered and ethnic differences, ignoring the way that abilities are measured by scholastic criteria which often stem not from natural 'gifts', but from 'the greater or lesser affinity between class cultural habits and the demands of the educational system or the criteria which define success within it' (Bourdieu and Passeron 1977: 22).

At Parkfield School, like so many schools in England, social reproduction persists and so too does social inequality (Hoskins and Barker 2014). Theresa May's plans to achieve equalised education provision and fair educational outcomes seems a distant reality in the current neo liberal, highly individualised education system that in practice, prioritises the success and opportunities of the privileged few over the success of the majority. Those young people whose identity does not fit the academic nature of twenty-first-century schooling in England may find themselves overlooked. Thus, we need to work together across political divisions to continue challenging inequalities related to class, gender and cultural differences to ensure a socially just education system that is varied, diverse and inclusive to enable all young people to fulfil their education and employment potential.

BIBLIOGRAPHY

Acker, S. (1994) *Gendered Education*. Buckingham: Open University Press.

Adams, R. J. (2001) Public Employment Relations: Canadian Developments in Perspective, in G. Swimmer. (ed) *Public-Sector Labour Relations in an Era of Restraint and Restructuring*. New York: Oxford University.

Aguilera-Barchet, B. (2012) *A Higher Education for the Twenty-first Century: European and US Approaches*. Brussels: Centre for European Studies.

Ainley, P., & Allen, M. (2010) *Lost Generation? New strategies for youth and education*. London: Continuum.

Alcock, R. (2011) 'Why universities are charging £9,000 fees; Economic theory shows universities are like champagne, not potatoes'. *The Guardian* 7 April. Online https://www.theguardian.com/education/mortarboard/2011/apr/07/tuition-fees-economic-theory (accessed 9 September 2015).

Allen, K. (2014) '"Blair's children': young women as 'aspirational subjects' in the psychic landscape of class" in *The Sociological Review*, Vol. 62 (4): 760–779.

Anxo, D., Bosch, G., & Rubery, J. (eds) (2010) *The Welfare State and Life Transitions: A European Perspective*. Gloucestershire: Edward Elgar Publishing Limited.

Archer, L., Halsall, A., & Hollingworth, S. (2007) 'Class, gender, (hetero)sexuality and schooling: paradoxes within working-class girls' engagement with education and post-16 aspirations' in *British Journal of Sociology of Education*, Vol. 28 (2): 165–180.

Archer, L., Mendick, H., & Hollingworth, S. (2010) *Urban Youth and Schooling*. Maidenhead: Open University Press.

© The Author(s) 2017
K. Hoskins, *Youth Identities, Education and Employment*,
Policy and Practice in the Classroom,
DOI 10.1057/978-1-137-35292-7

Archer, L., & Hutchings, M. (2000) '"Bettering Yourself"? Discourses of Risk, Cost and Benefit in Ethnically Diverse, Young Working-Class Non-Participants' Constructions of Higher Education" in *British Journal of Sociology of Education*, Vol. 21 (4): 555–574.

Archer, L., & Yamashita, H. (2003) 'Knowing their limits'? Identities, Inequalities and Inner City School Leavers' Post-16 Aspirations' in *Journal of Education Policy*, Vol. 18 (1): 53–69.

Arnot, M. (2008) *Educating the Female Citizen*. London: Taylor and Francis.

Ashworth, A., Hardman, J., Woon-Chia, L., Maguire, S., Middleton, S., Dearden, L., Emmerson, C., Frayne, C., Goodman, A., Ichimura, H., & Meghir, C. (2001) *Education Maintenance Allowance: The First Year. A Quantitative Evaluation*. London: DfE RR257.

Avis, J. (2014) 'Comfort radicalism and NEETs: a conservative praxis' in in *International Studies in Sociology of Education*, Vol. 24 (3): 272–289.

Ball, S., Maguire, M., & Macrae, S. (2000) *Choice, Pathways and Transitions Post-16: New Youth, New Economies in the Global City*. London: Routledge Falmer.

Ball, S. J. (2003) *Class Strategies and the Education Market: The Middle Classes and Social Advantage*. London: RoutledgeFalmer.

Ball, S. J. (2012) *The Micro-Politics of the School: Towards a Theory of School Organization*. Oxon: Routledge.

Ball, S. J. (2016) *Labouring to Relate: Neoliberalism, Embodied Policy and Network Dynamics*. Peabody, MA: PEA Yearbook.

Banyuls, J., & Recio, A. (2012) Spain: The nightmare of Mediterranean neoliberalism, in S. Lehndorff. (ed.) *A Triumph of Failed Ideas: European Models of Capitalism in Crisis*. Brussels: ETUI, 199–218.

Barker, B., & Hoskins, K. (2015) 'Can High Performing Academies Overcome Family Background and Improve Social Mobility?' in *British Journal of Sociology of Education*. doi:10.1080/01425692.2015.1073104.

Basit, T., & And Modood, T. (2016) Ethnic Capital, Higher Education and Life Chances, in J. Cote & A. Furlong. (eds) *Oxford Handbook of Higher Education*. Oxford: Oxford University Press.

Bassey, M. (1999) *Case Study Research in Educational Settings. Doing Qualitative Research in Educational Settings*. Buckingham: Open University Press.

Bathmaker, A.-M., Ingram, N., Abrahams, J., Hoare, A., Waller, R. and Bradley, H. (2016) *Higher Education, Social Class and Social Mobility: The Degree Generation*. London: Palgrave Macmillan.

Bathmaker, A.-M., Ingram, N., & Waller, R. (2013) 'Higher Education, Social Class and The Mobilisation of Capitals: Recognising and Playing the Game' in *British Journal of Sociology of Education*, Vol. 34 (5-6): 723–743.

Bauman, Z. (2005) *Liquid Life*. Cambridge: Policy Press.

BBC (2011) 'Q&A: EMA grants'. *BBC 28 March*. Online: (http://www.bbc.co.uk/news/education-12209072, (accessed 5 August 2015).

BBC Science (2013) 'The Great British Class Survey – Results'. *BBC* 3 April. Online www.bbc.co.uk/science/0/21970879 (accessed 17 May 2013).

Beare, H., Caldwell, B., & Millikan, R. (1989) *Creating an excellent school.* London: Routledge.

Beck, U. (1998) *World Risk Society.* Cambridge: Polity Press.

Berger, P., & Luckmann, T. (1966) *The Social Construction of Reality: A Treatise in the Sociology of Knowledge.* New York: Random House.

Bishop, D. (2016) 'Clarity of purpose in the TEF and the REF', *Times Higher Education.* Online: https://www.timeshighereducation.com/blog/clarity-pur pose-tef-and-ref (accessed 9 January 2017).

Blanchflower, D. G., & Freeman, R. B. (eds) (2000) *Youth Employment and Joblessness in Advanced Countries.* Chicago: University of Chicago Press.

Blanden, J., & Machin, S. (2007) 'Recent Changes in Intergenerational Mobility in Britain', *The Sutton Trust.* Online: http://www.suttontrust.com/wp-con tent/uploads/2007/12/intergenerationalmobilityinukfull.pdf (accessed 20 July 2015).

Blunkett, D. (2008) *The Inclusive Society: Social mobility in 21st century Britain.* London: Progress.

Boffey, D. (2015) Youth unemployment rate is worst for 20 years, compared with overall figure. *The Guardian* 21 February. Online https://www.theguardian. com/society/2015/feb/22/youth-unemployment-jobless-figure, (accessed 31 August 2016).

Bourdieu, P. (1977) *Outline of a Theory of Practice.* Cambridge: Cambridge University Press.

Bourdieu, P. (1990) *The Logic of Practice.* Cambridge: Polity.

Bourdieu, P. (1993) *Sociology in Question.* London: Sage.

Bourdieu, P. (ed) (1999) Job insecurity is everywhere now, in *Acts of Resistance: Against the Tyranny of the Market.* New York: New Press.

Bourdieu, P., & Passeron, J. C. (1977) *Reproduction in Education, Society and Culture.* London: Sage.

Bourdieu, P., & Wacquant, L. (1992) *An invitation to reflexive sociology.* Chicago: University of Chicago Press.

Bowl, M., & Hughes, T. (2014) 'Fair access and fee setting in English universities: what do institutional statements suggest about university stra tegies in a stratified quasi-market?' in in *Studies in Higher Education,* Vol. 41 (2): 269–287.

Bowles, S., & Gintis, H. (1976) *Schooling in Capitalist America: Education Reform and the Contradictions of Economic Life.* New York: Basic Books Inc.

Bradley, H., & Ingram, N. (2013) Banking on the Future: choices, aspirations and economic hardship in working-class student experience, in W. Atkinson, S. Roberts, & M. Savage. (eds) *Class Inequality in Austerity Britain.* Basingstoke: Palgrave Macmillan.

Brah, A., & Phoenix, A. (2004) 'Ain't I A Woman? Revisiting Intersectionality' in *Journal of International Women's Studies*, Vol. 5 (3): 75–86.

Bratti, M., McKnight, A., Naylor, R., & Smith, J. (2004) 'Higher Education Outcomes, Graduate Employment and University Performance Indicators' in in *Journal of the Royal Statistical Society*, Vol. 167 (3): 475–496.

Brignall, M., & Timms, A. (2015) 'EasyJet - the airline that's difficult to deal with'. *The Guardian* 5 December. Online: https://www.theguardian.com/business/2015/dec/05/easyjet-complaints-compensation-claims-denied (accessed 12 December 2015).

British Educational Research Association (BERA) (2011) *Revised Ethical Guidelines For Educational Research*. Online: https://www.bera.ac.uk/wp-content/uploads/2014/02/BERA-Ethical-Guidelines-2011.pdf?noredirect=1, (accessed 5 January 2014).

British Sociological Association (BSA) (2002) *Statement of Ethical Practice*. Online:www.britsoc.co.uk/user_doc/Statement%20of%20Ethical%20Practice.pdf (accessed 1 March 2014).

Brooks, R. (2007) 'Young People's Extra-Curricular Activities: Critical Social Engagement – Or 'Something for the CV'?' in *Journal of Social Policy*, Vol. 36 (3): 417–434.

Brown, P., Lauder, H., & Ashton, D. (2011) *The Global Auction: The Broken Promises of Education, Jobs, and Incomes*. Oxford: Oxford University Press.

Brown, P., & Lauder, H. (2012) *Education: In Search of A Future*. London: Routledge.

Brown, P., & Lauder, H. (2013) 'Auctioning the future of work' in in *World Policy Journal*, Vol. 30 (2): 16–25.

Buck, T. (2014) 'Spanish youth in crisis'. *Financial Times* 23 May. Online: https://www.ft.com/content/5908da36-db09-11e3-8273-00144feabdc0 (accessed 5 January 2016).

Burgen, S. (2013) 'Spain youth unemployment reaches record 56.1%'. *The Guardian* 30 August. Online: https://www.theguardian.com/business/2013/aug/30/spain-youth-unemployment-record-high (accessed 10 March 2014).

Burke, P. J. (2012) *The Right to Higher Education: Beyond widening participation*. London: Routledge.

Burke, P. J. (2013) 'Formations of Masculinity and Higher Education Pedagogies' in *Culture, Society and Masculinities*, Vol. 5 (2): 109–126.

Burr, V. (2003) *Social Constructionism*. East Sussex: Routledge.

Butler, J. (2004) *Precarious Life: The Powers of Mourning and Violence*. London and New York: Verso.

Butler, J. (2008) *Judith Butler in conversation: analyzing the texts and talk of everyday life*. London: Routledge.

Butler, J. (2009) *Frames of war: when is life grievable?*. London, New York: Verso.

Calhoun, C., LiPuma, E., & Postone, M. (eds) (1993) *Bourdieu: Critical Perspectives*. Cambridge: Polity.

Callender, C. (2003) Student financial support in higher education: access and exclusion, in M. Tight. (ed.) *Access and Exclusion (International Perspectives on Higher Education Research*. Bradford: Emerald Group Publishing Limited, 127–158.

Callender, C., & Jackson, J. (2008) 'Does the fear of debt constrain choice of university and subject of study?' in *Studies in Higher Education*, Vol. 33 (4): 405–429.

Chevalier, A., & Conlon, G. (2003) *Does it pay to attend a prestigious university?*. London: Centre for the Economics of Education.

Chowdry, H., Dearden, L., & Emerson, K. (2008) *Education Maintenance Allowance evaluation with administrative data*. London: Learning and Skills Council National Office.

Chowdry, H., & Emerson, K. (2010) *An efficient maintenance allowance?*. London: Institute for Fiscal Studies.

City and Guilds Group (2016) *The Economic Benefits of vocational education and training in the UK*. Online: https://www.cityandguildsgroup.com/~/media/CGG%20Website/Documents/CGGroupUK%20pdf.ashx (accessed 10 August 2016).

Codiroli, N. (2015) 'Inequalities in students' choice of STEM subjects: An exploration of intersectional relationships'. *CLS working paper*. London: Centre for Longitudinal Studies.

Cohen, P. (2006) 'Re-doing the Knowledge: Labour, Learning and Life Knowledge in Transit' in *Journal of Education and Work*, Vol. 19 (2): 109–120.

Coleman, J. C. (1988) 'Social capital in the creation of human capital' in *American Journal of Sociology*, Vol. 94: 95–120.

Coleman, J. C. (1994) *Foundations of Social Theory*. Cambridge, Mass.: Harvard University Press.

Coughlan, S. (2013) 'More jobs for graduates than the unqualified in UK – study'. *BBC* 24 April. Online: http://www.bbc.co.uk/news/education-22268809 (accessed 5 May, 2013).

Cree, V. E. (ed.) (2013) *Social Work: A Reader*. Oxon: Routledge.

Croll, P. (2004) 'Families, Social Capital and Educational Outcomes' in *British Journal of Educational Studies*, Vol. 52 (4): 390–416.

Croxford, L., Iannelli, C., Shapira, M., Howieson, C., & Raffe, D. (2006) *Education and Youth Transitions across Britain 1984-2002, CES Briefing No. 39*. Edinburgh: Centre for Educational Sociology, University of Edinburgh.

Croxford, L., & Raffe, D. (2014) 'Social class, ethnicity and access to higher education in the four countries of the UK: 1996-2010' in *International Journal of Lifelong Education*, Vol. 33 (1): 77–95.

Crozier, G., Bhopal, K., & Devine, D. (2010) "Race', Education and Globalisation' in Irish Educational Studies Journal, Special Issue, Vol. 29 (3): 207–212.

Crozier, G., & Reay, D. (2011) 'Capital Accumulation: Working Class Students Learning How to Learn in *Higher Education*' in *Teaching in Higher Education Journal*, Vol. 16 (2): 145–155.

David, M., & Naidoo, R. (eds) (2012) *The Sociology of Higher Education: Reproduction, Transformation and Change in a Global Era*. London: Routledge.

Davies, P., Slack, K., Hughes, A., Mangan, J., & Vigurs, K. (2008) *Knowing Where to Study? Fees, Bursaries and Fair Access*. Staffordshire: Staffordshire University Press.

Davis, D., Bryant, J. L., & Zaharieva, J. (2012) Leadership Relationships Between Centre Directors and University Administrators in Cooperative Research Centres: A Multilevel Analysis, in C. Boardman, D. O. Gray, & R. Drew. (eds) *Cooperative Research Centers and Technical Innovation: Government Policies*. London/New York: Springer.

Dearing, R. (1997) *Higher education in the learning society, Report of the National Committee of Enquiry into Higher Education*. London: HMSO.

Deem, R., Hillyard, S., & Reed, M. (2007) Knowledge, higher education, and the new managerialism: The changing management of UK universities. Oxford: Oxford University Press.

Department for Business, Innovation and Skills (2015) 'Graduate Labour Market Statistics: 2015'. *DfBIS*. Online: https://www.gov.uk/government/uploads/system/uploads/attachment_data/file/518654/bis-16-232-graduate-labour-market-statistics-2015.pdf (accessed 5 January 2016).

Department for Education (2011) 'NEET Statistics: Quarterly Brief - Quarter 4 2010'. *DfE*. Online: http://www.education.gov.uk/rsgateway/DB/STR/d000987/index.shtml (accessed 22 June 2014).

Derrick, J., Gawn, J., & Ecclestone, K. (2008) 'Evaluating the 'spirit' and 'letter' of formative assessment in the learning cultures of part-time adult literacy and numeracy classes' in *Research Issues in Post-Compulsory Education*, Vol. 13 (2): 173–184.

Devine, F. (2004) *Class Practices: How parents help their children get good jobs*. Cambridge: Cambridge University Press.

Dorling, D. (2014) *Inequality and the 1%*. London: Verso Books.

Doward, J., & Ratcliffe, R. (2016) 'Quarter of UK graduates are low earners 10 years after university'. *The Guardian* 13 August. Online: https://www.theguardian.com/education/2016/aug/13/quarter-of-graduates-are-low-earners (accessed 12 September 2016).

Dunnett, A., Moorhouse, J., Walsh, C., & Barry, C. (2012) 'Choosing a University: A Conjoint Analysis of the Impact of Higher Fees on Students Applying for University in 2012' in *Tertiary Education and Management*, Vol. 18 (3): 199–220.

Ecclestone, K., Biesta, G., Hughes, M. (eds) (2009) *Transitions and Learning through the London*, Routledge, p. 1–15.

Elliott, L. (2010) 'Jobless total rises above 2.5m as public-sector cull begins'. *The Guardian* 16 December. Online: https://www.theguardian.com/business/2010/dec/16/jobless-total-rises-public-sector (accessed 5 July 2015).

Elwood, J. (2016) Gender and the Curriculum, in D. Wyse, L. Hayward, & J. Pandya. (eds) *The SAGE Handbook of Curriculum, Pedagogy and Assessment*. London: Sage.

Epstein, D., Elwood, J., Hey, V., & Maw, J. (eds) (1998) *Failing Boys? Issues in Gender and Education*. Buckingham: Open University Press.

European Union Committee (2012) 'TVET and Skills Development in E. U. Development Cooperation'. *European Commission*. Online: http://ec.europa.eu/europeaid/sites/devco/files/tvet-study-aets-2012-final-report_en.pdf (accessed 5 July 2015).

Evans, J., & Shen, W. (eds) (2010) *Youth Employment and the Future of Work*. Strasbourg: Council of Europe Publishing.

Francis, B. (2000) *Boys, Girls and Achievement: Addressing the classroom issues*. London: Routledge Falmer.

Francis, B. (2006) 'An Investigation of the Discourses Children Draw on Their Constructions of Gender' in *Journal of Applied Social Psychology*, Vol. 29 (2): 300–316.

Francis, B., Skelton, C., & Read, B. (2010) 'The simultaneous production of educational achievement and popularity: how do some pupils accomplish it?' in *British Educational Research Journal*, Vol. 36 (2): 317–340.

Francis, B., Skelton, C., & Read, B. (2012) *Identities and practices of high achieving pupils: negotiating achievement and peer cultures*. London: Bloomsbury Publishing.

Fraser, N. (1997) *Justice Interrupts: Critical Reflections on the "Postsocialist" Condition*. New York: Routledge.

Fuller, A., Heath, S., Dyke, M., Foskett, N., Foskett, R., Johnston, B., Maringe, F., Rice, P., & Taylor, J. (2006) Non-Participation in Higher Education: Decisionmaking as an embedded social practice ESRC TLRP. Online. http://www.tlrp.org/proj/wphe/wp_fuller.html (accessed October 2014).

Fuller, A., Foskett, R., Johnston, B., Paton, K., & Thomas, K. (2011) in. (eds) *Gendered Choices: Learning, Work, Identities in Lifelong Learning*. London: Springer189–208.

Gaine, C. (1995) *Still No Problem Here*. Staffordshire: Trentham Books Ltd.

Galley, D. (2014) 'Why are there so few male social workers?' *The Guardian* 5 July. Online: https://www.theguardian.com/social-carenetwork/2014/jul/25/why-so-few-male-social-workers (accessed 17 March 2015).

General Teaching Council for England (GTCE) (2011) 'Annual digest of statistics 2010–11 Profiles of registered teachers in England'. *GTCE* Online: http://dera.ioe.ac.uk/11914/1/annual_digest_psd110811.pdf (accessed 5 April 2016).

Gewirtz, S. (1998) 'Conceptualizing social justice in education: mapping the territory' in *Journal of Education Policy*, Vol. 13 (4): 469–484.

Gewirtz, S. (2001) 'Cloning the Blairs: New Labour's programme for the re-socialisation of working-class parents' in *Journal of Education Policy*, Vol. 16 (4): 365–378.

Gewirtz, S., & Cribb, A. (2002) 'Plural conceptions of social justice: implications for policy sociology' in *Journal of Education Policy*, Vol. 17 (5): 499–509.

Giddens, A. (1991) *Modernity and Self-Identity*. Cambridge: Polity Press.

Gillborn, D. (2013) 'Interest-divergence and the colour of cutbacks: race, recession and the undeclared war on Black children' in *Discourse: Studies in the Cultural Politics of Education*, Vol. 34 (4): 477–491.

Gouvias, D. (2012) 'Accountability in the Greek Higher Education System as a High-Stakes Policymaking Instrument' in *Higher Education Policy*, Vol. 25 (1): 65–86.

Gove, M. (2011a) 'The moral purpose of school reform'. Address at the National College for School Leadership, Birmingham, 16 June. Online. www.education.gov.uk/inthenews/speeches/a0077859/the-moral-purpose-of-school-reform (accessed 6 January 2017).

Gove, M. (2011b) 'Oral statement on the schools White Paper'. Department for Education, 9 February. Online: www.education.gov.uk/schools/toolsandinitiatives/schoolswhitepaper/a0068680/oral-statement (accessed 6 January 2017).

Gunderson, M., & Fazio, F. (eds) (2014) *Tackling Youth Unemployment*. Cambridge: Cambridge Scholars Publishing.

Hall, S. (1990) Cultural identity and diaspora, in J. Rutherford. *Identity: community, culture, difference*. London: Lawrence & Wishart.

Halsey, A. H., Heath, A. F., & Ridge, J. M. (1980) *Origins and Destinations*. Oxford: Clarendon Press.

Hamilton, L., & Corbett-Whittier, C. (2013) *Using Case Study in Education Research*. London: Sage.

Hartas, D. (2012) 'Inequality and the home learning environment: predications about seven year olds' language and literacy' in *British Educational Research Journal*, Vol. 38 (5): 859–879.

Harvey, D. (2005) *A Brief History of Neoliberalism*. Oxford: Oxford University Press.

Heathfield, M., & Fusco, D. (eds) (2015) *Youth and Inequality in Education: Global Actions in Youth Work*. Oxon: Routledge.

Hermann, C. (2013) 'Crisis, Structural Reform and the Dismantling of the European Social Model(s)'. IPE Working Paper 26/2013. Berlin: Institute for International Political Economy.

Hermann, C. (2015) 'Crisis and social policy in Europe' in *Global Social Policy*, Vol. 15 (1): 82–85.

Hey, V. (2003) Identification and mortification in late modernity: New Labour; alpha feminities & their dis/contents. Keynote Address at the *2003 International Conference of Gender and Education*. University of Sheffield.

Higher Education Funding Council for England (HEFCE) (2015) '£1.6 million HEFCE Catalyst funding for higher apprenticeships in partnership with business'. *HEFCE* 16 July. Online: http://www.hefce.ac.uk/news/newsarchive/2015/Name,104718,en.html (accessed 3 March 2016).

Higher Education Statistics Agency (HESA) (2012) 'What do graduates do? Career planning for higher education and beyond. *HESA*. Online: http://www.hecsu.ac.uk/assets/assets/documents/WDGD_Oct_2012.pdf (accessed 1 January 2013).

HM Government. (2009) *New Opportunitites: Fair chances for the future*. CM 7533. Norwich: The Stationery Office.

HM Government (2010) *Unleashing Aspiration: The government response to the final report of the panel on fair access to the professions*. CM7755. London: The Stationery Office.

HM Government. (2016) *English Apprenticeships: Our 2020 Vision*. London: The Stationery Office.

Hodkinson, P., Sparkes, A. C., & Hodkinson, H. (1996) *Triumphs and Tears: Young People, Markets and the Transition from School to Work*. London: David Fulton.

Holdsworth, C. (2010) 'Why Volunteer? Understanding Motivations For Student Volunteering' in *British Journal of Educational Studies*, Vol. 58 (4): 421–437.

Hoskins, K. (2012) 'Widening participation aims and outcomes: examining higher education prospects for four non-traditional students' in Widening Participation and Lifelong Learning, Vol. 14 (3): 235–249.

Hoskins, K., & Ball, S. (2017) Education and Social Class, in A. Van Zanten. (ed.) Dictionnaire de l'éducation. Quadridge/ PUF.

Hoskins, K., & Barker, B. (2014) *Education and Social Mobility: Dreams of Success*. London/Staffordshire: IOE and Trentham Books.

Hoskins, K., & Barker, B. (2016) 'Aspirations, social mobility and social reproduction: young people's constructions of their future careers' in *British Journal of Education Studies*. doi:http://dx.doi.org/10.1080/00071005.2016.1182616.

Hoskins, K., & Ille, S. (2016) Widening Participation to under-represented and disadvantaged students; contextual barriers to learning and academic success, in M. Shah & G. Whiteford. (eds) *Bridges, Pathways and Transitions: International Innovations in Widening Participation*. Cambridge, MA: Chandos/Elsevier.

House of Commons Library (2012) 'Participation by 16-19 year olds in education and training'. *Parliament*. HoCL Online: http://www.publications.parliament.uk/pa/cm201012/cmselect/cmeduc/850/85006.htm (accessed 5 January, 2013).

House of Commons Library (2016) 'HE in England from 2012: Funding and finance', Briefing Paper Number 6206 29 January. *HoCL* Online file:///C:/Users/Damienand/Downloads/SN06206%20(1).pdf (accessed 1 August 2016).

Hussein, I., McNally, S., & Telhaj, S. (2009) 'University Quality and Graduate Wages in the UK'. *Centre for the Economics of Education CEE DP 99*. Online: http://cee.lse.ac.uk/ceedps/ceedp99.pdf (accessed 5 January, 2013).

Independent Commission on Fees (2014) 'Analysis of trends in higher education applications, admissions, and enrolments'. *ICoF* Online: http://www.indepen dentcommissionfees.org.uk/wordpress/wp-content/uploads/2014/08/ ICoF-Report-Aug-2014.pdf (accessed 5 November 2015).

Jackson, B., & Marsden, D. (1962) *Education and the working class: some general themes raised by a study of 88 working class children in a Northern industrial city.* London: Routledge.

James, D. (2015) 'How Bourdieu bites back: recognising misrecognition in education and educational research' in *Cambridge Journal of Education*, Vol. 45 (1): 97–112.

Jenkins, R. (1992) *Key Sociologists; Pierre Bourdieu.* New York: Routledge.

Jones, K. (2014) 'Conservatism and educational crisis: the case of England' in in *Education Inquiry*, Vol. 5 (1): 89–108.

Jones, K. (2015) *Education in Britain: 1944 to the Present* (2nd). Cambridge: Polity Press.

Karamessini, M. (2010) 'Labour market impact of four recessions on women and men in Greece: Comparative analysis in a long term perspective' In *Social Cohesion and Development*, Vol. 7 (2): 3–104.

Kenway, J., Willis, S., Blackmore, J., & Rennie, L. (1998) *Answering back: Girls, boys and feminism in school.* London: Routledge.

Labour Force Survey (2013) 'User Guide VOLUME 3'. *Office for National Statistics* February. Online: vol32013v1odforweb_tcm77-311300 (1).pdf (accessed 22 October 2014).

Ladson-Billings, G. (2006) They're trying to wash us away: The adolescence of critical race theory in education, in A. D. Dixson & C. K. Rousseau. (eds) *Critical race theory in education: All God's children got a song.* New York: Routledge.

Lanning, T., & Rudiger, K. (2012) 'Youth unemployment in Europe: lessons for the UK', *TUC, cipd and IPPR*. Online: https://www.researchonline.org.uk/ sds/search/download.do%3Bjsessionid=8EB0BC2ACB0 9A1B9DD9ED6AA24C78047?ref=B27130 (accessed 22 October 2014).

Lareau, A. (2004) *Unequal Childhoods: Class, Race and Family Life.* Berkeley: University of California Press.

Lauder, H., Brown, P., & Halsey, A. H. (2010) The sociology of education as 'redemption': A critical history, in J. Furlong & M. Lawn. (eds) *Disciplines of Education.* London: Routledge, 13–30.

Leatz, C. A. (1993) *Career Success/Personal Stress.* London: McGraw-Hill Inc.

Leschke, J., Watt, A., & Finn, M. (2012) Job quality in the crisis – an update of the Job Quality Index (JQI)', in *European Trade Union Institute.* Working Paper 2012.07

Levy, C., & Hopkins, L. (2010) 'Shaping Up for Innovation: Are we delivering the right skills for the 2020 knowledge economy?'. *The Work Foundation - A Knowledge Economy programme report.* Online: http://www.theworkfounda tion.com/assets/docs/publications/262_Shaping_up_for_Innovation.pdf (accessed 22 October 2014).

Li, H. (2013) "Rural Students' Experiences in a Chinese Elite University: Capital, Habitus and Practices' in *British Journal of Sociology of Education*, Vol. 34: 829–847.

Lillicot, A. (2016) 'Theresa May's 'meritocracy' is a recipe for Darwinian dystopia'. *The Telegraph* 12 September. Online: http://www.telegraph.co.uk/ news/2016/09/12/theresa-mays-meritocracy-is-a-recipe-for-darwinian-dysto pia/, accessed 1 October 2016.

Lillis, T. M. (2001) *Student writing: access, regulation, desire.* London: Routledge.

Ling, T. J., & O'Brien, K. M. (2012) "Connecting the forgotten half: The school-to-work transition of noncollege-bound youth' in *Journal of Career Development*, Vol. 40: 347–367.

Longitudinal Education Outcomes (LEO) (2016) 'Employment and Earnings Outcomes of Higher Education Graduates: Experimental data from the Longitudinal Education Outcomes (LEO) dataset', *Department for Education.* Online: https://www.gov.uk/government/uploads/system/ uploads/attachment_data/file/543794/SFR36-2016_main_text_LEO.pdf (accessed 1 September, 2016).

Maguire, M. (1997) Missing Links; Working-Class Women of Irish Descent, in P. Mahony & C. Zmroczek. (eds) Class Matters: 'Working Class' Women's Perspectives on Social Class. London: Taylor & Francis, 87–100.

Maguire, M., Perryman, J., Ball, S., & Braun, A. (2011) 'The ordinary school - what is it?' in *British Journal of Sociology of Education*, Vol. 32 (1): 1–16.

Marseilles, M. (2010) 'Greece: an expensive free education'. *University World News* 24 January. Online: (http://www.universityworldnews.com/article. php?story=2010012409184186, (accessed 16 November).

McCann, D. (2010) *The Political Economy of the European Union: An Institutionalist Perspective.* Cambridge: Polity.

McCrone, T., Gardiner, C., Southcott, C., & Featherstone, G. (2010) 'Information, Advice and Guidance for Young People (LG Group Research Report)', *NFER.* Online: http://www.nfer.ac.uk/publications/LIAG01 (accessed, 16 June 2014).

McDowell, L. (2011) *Capital culture: Gender at work in the city.* Oxford: Blackwell Publishers Limited.

McNay, L. (1996) *Gender, habitus and the field: Pierre Bourdieu and the limits of reflexivity.* Paper presented at the Institute of Advanced Legal Studies, May 1996.

Medway, P., Rhodes, V., Macrae, S., Maguire, M., & Gewirtz, S. (2003) *Widening Participation through Supporting Undergraduates: what is being done and what can be done to support student progression at King's?*. London: King's College Department of Education and Professional Studies.

Mendick, H., Allen, K., & Harvey, L. (2015) '"We can Get Everything We Want if We Try Hard": Young People, Celebrity, Hard Work' in *British Journal of Educational Studies*, Vol. 63 (2): 161–178.

Mendick, M. (2005) 'A beautiful myth? The gendering of being/doing 'good at maths" in *Gender and Education*, Vol. 17 (2): 203–219.

Mills, C. (2008) 'Reproduction and transformation of inequalities in schooling: the transformative potential of the theoretical constructs of Bourdieu' in in *British Journal of Sociology of Education*, Vol. 29 (1): 79–89.

Mirza, H. (2009) *Race, gender and educational desire: why Black women succeed and fail*. London: Routledge.

Modood, T., Berthoud, R., Lakey, J., Nazroo, J., Smith, P., Virdee, S., & Beishon, S. (1997) *Ethnic Minorities in Britain: Diversity and Disadvantage*. London: Policy.

Moore, R. (2012) Education, Production and Reform, in P. Brown & H. Lauder. (ed) *Education: In Search of A Future*. London: Routledge, 99–130.

Morgan, D. L. (1988) *Focus Groups as Qualitative Research*. California: Sage Publications Limited.

Nash, R. (1999) 'Bourdieu, 'Habitus', and Educational Research; is it all worth the candle?' in *British Journal of Sociology of Education*, Vol. 20 (2). 175–187.

National Union of Teachers (NUT) (2012) 142nd Annual Report. NUT Online: https://www.teachers.org.uk/files/Annual-Report-2012.pdf (accessed 6 January 2017).

National Association of Colleges and Employers. (2014) *The Class of 2014 Student Survey Report*. NACE. Online: http://career.sa.ucsb.edu/files/docs/hand outs/2014-student-survey.pdf (accessed 2 May 2017).

Navarro, Z. (2006) 'In Search of Cultural Interpretation of Power' in *IDS Bulletin*, Vol. 37 (6): 11–22.

Nölke, A. (2016) 'Economic causes of the Eurozone crisis: the analytical contribution of Comparative Capitalism' in *Socio-Economic Review*, Vol. 14 (1): 141–161.

O'Leary, N., & Sloane, P. (2005) 'The Return to a University Education in Great Britain' in *National Institute Economic Review*, Vol. 193: 75–89.

O'Neill, M. (2016) *Youth Unemployment Statistics*. House of Commons Briefing Paper 5871.

Office for Fair Access (OFFA) (2014) 'Trends in young participation by student background and selectivity of institution'. *OFFA* Online: www.offa.org.uk/publications (accessed 27 September, 2016).

Office for Standards in Education, Children's Services and Skills (OFSTED) (2015) 'Apprenticeships: developing skills for future prosperity'. OFSTED Online: https://www.gov.uk/government/publications/apprenticeships-developing-skills-for-future-prosperity (accessed 6 January 2017).

Ong, A.. (2006) *Neoliberalism as Exception: Mutations in Citizenship and Sovereignty*. North Carolina: Duke University Press.

Ong, A. (2007) 'Neoliberalism as a mobile technology' in *Transactions of the Institute of British Geographers*, Vol. 32 (1): 3–8.

Open University (2016) 'Fees and Funding'. *OU* Online: http://www.open.ac.uk/postgraduate/fees-and-funding (accessed 27 September 2016).

Osborne, H. (2012) 'Graduate unemployment levels on a par with school leavers'. *The Guardian* 22 February Online: https://www.theguardian.com/money/2012/feb/22/graduates-unemployment-levels-school-leavers (accessed 1 July 2014).

Peever, C. (2013) 'Students demand reinstatement of EMA'. *The Independent* 28 February. Online: http://www.independent.co.uk/student/news/students-demand-reinstatement-of-ema-8514373.html (accessed March 2015).

Phillips, M. (2010) Rural community vitality and malaise: moving beyond the rhetoric, in ESRC/Scottish Government (ed.) *Rural community empowerment in the 21st century: building a 'can-do' culture*. Swindon: ESRC.

Policy Forum (2015) 'Social mobility and education - school choice, character education and the Pupil Premium', in http://www.westminsterforumprojects.co.uk/forums/event.php?eid=1067 (accessed 5 January, 2016).

Power, S., Edwards, T., Whitty, G., & Wigfall, V. (2003) *Education and the Middle Classes*. Buckingham: Open University Press.

Power, S., & Gewirtz, S. (2001) 'Reading Education Action Zones' in *Journal of Education Policy*, Vol. 16 (1): 39–51.

Power, S., & Whitty, G. (2006) Education and the Middle Class: A Complex But Crucial Case for the Sociology of Education, in H. Lauder, P. Brown, J. Dillabough, & A. Halsey. (eds) *Education, Globalization and Social Change*. Oxford: Oxford University Press, 446–453.

Punch, K. (2009) *Introduction to Research Methods in Education*. London: Sage.

Putnam, R. (2000) *Bowling Alone: The Collapse and Revival of American Community*. New York: Simon and Schuster.

Putnam, R. (2001) "Social Capital: Measurement and Consequences' in *Isuma: Canadian Journal of Policy Research*, Vol. Vol.2: 41–51.

Putnam, R. D. (1995) 'Bowling Alone: America's Declining Social Capital' in *Journal of Democracy*, Vol. 6 (1): 65–78.

Radice, H. (2013) 'How we got here: UK higher education under neoliberalism' in *ACME: An International E-Journal for Critical Geographies*, Vol. 12 (3): 407–441.

Ratcliffe, R. (2012) 'Why should I study at a Russell Group university?' *The Guardian* 19 December. Online: http://www.theguardian.com/education/2012/dec/19/should-i-go-to-a-russell-group-university (accessed 10 January 2016).

Reay, D. (1997) 'Feminist theory, habitus, and social class: disrupting notions of classlessness' in *Women's Studies International Forum*, Vol. 20 (2): 225–233.

Reay, D. (2001) 'Finding or losing yourself?: working-class relationships to education' in *Journal of Education Policy*, Vol. 16 (4): 1–14.

Reay, D. (2004) "It's all becoming a habitus': beyond the habitual use of habitus in educational research' in *British Journal of Sociology of Education*, Vol. 25 (4): 431–444.

Reay, D., David, M., & Ball, S. J. (2005) *Degrees of Choice: social class, race and gender in higher education*. Staffordshire: Trentham Books Limited.

Reay, D. (2005) 'Beyond Consciousness?: The Psychic Landscape of Social Class' in *Sociology Special Issue of Class, Culture and Identity*, Vol. 39 (5): 911–928.

Reay, D. (2006) 'The Zombie Stalking English Schools: Social Class and Educational Inequality' in *British Journal of Educational Studies*, Vol. 54 (3): 288–307.

Reay, D., Crozier, G., & Clayton, J. (2010) '"Fitting in" or "standing out': working-class students in UK higher education' in *British Educational Research Journal*, Vol. 32 (1): 1–19.

Reay, D., Crozier, G., & James, D. (2013) 'White Middle-class Identities and Urban Schooling' in *British Journal of Educational Studies*, Vol. 62 (2): 249–252.

Reed, L. R., Gates, P., & Last, K. (2007) *Young Participation in Higher Education in the Parliamentary Constituencies of Birmingham Hodge Hill, Bristol South, Nottingham North and Sheffield Brightside*. Bristol: UWE and HEFCE.

Rhodes, R. A. W. (1994) 'The Hollowing out of the State: The Changing Nature of the State in Britain' in *Political Quarterly*, Vol. 65 (2): 138–151.

Riddell, S. (2012) *Gender and the Politics of the Curriculum*. London: Routledge.

Roberts, J. (2009) 'The global knowledge economy in question' in *Critical perspectives on international business*, Vol. 5 (4): 285–303.

Roberts, S., & Evans, S. (2013) 'Aspirations' and Imagined Futures: The Im/ possibilities for Britain's Young Working Class, in W. Atkinson, S. Roberts, & M. Savage. (eds) *Class Inequality in Austerity Britain*. Basingstoke: Palgrave Macmillan UK, 70–89.

Rollock, N., Gillborn, D., Vincent, C., & Ball, S. J. (2014) *The Colour of Class The Educational Strategies of the Black Middle Classes*. London: Routledge.

Searle, R., Erdogan, B., Peiró, J. M., & Klehe, U. C. (2014) 'What We Know About Youth Employment: Research Summary and Best Practices'. *Society for Industrial and Organizational Psychology*. Online: http://www.siop.org/ WhitePapers/Youth%20Employment%20Full%20FINAL.pdf (accessed 2 March 2016).

Shiner, M., & Noden, P. (2014) '"Why are you applying there?' 'Race', class and the construction of higher education 'choice' in the United Kingdom' in *British Journal of Sociology of Education*, Vol. 36 (8): 1–22.

Sinfield, S., Burns, T., & Holley, D. (2003) 'Outsiders Looking in or Insiders Looking out? Widening Participation in a Post 1992 University'. Paper presented at Discourse, Power & Resistance. Plymouth University, UK.

Skeggs, B. (1997) *Formations of class and gender: becoming respectable*. London: Sage.

Skelton, C. (2002) 'The "feminisation of schooling" or "re-masculinising" primary education?' in International Studies in *Sociology of Education*, Vol. 12 (1): 77–96.

Skelton, C., & Francis, B. (2009) *Feminism and the Schooling Scandal*. London: Routledge.

Social Exclusion Unit. (1999) *Bridging the Gap: New Opportunities for 16-18 Year Olds*. London: The Stationery Office.

Social Mobility and Child Poverty Commission (2015) State of the Nation 2015: Social Mobility and Child Poverty in Great Britain. Online: https://www.gov.uk/government/uploads/system/uploads/attachment_data/file/485926/State_of_the_nation_2015social_mobility_and_child_poverty_in_Great_Britain.pdf (accessed 3 January 2016).

Stahl, G. (2015) *Identity, neoliberalism and aspiration in white working-class boys: educating white working-class boys*. USA: Taylor and Francis.

Stein, M. (2005) *Resilience and Young People Leaving Care: Overcoming the odds*. Joseph Rowntree Foundation: York.

Stobart, G. (2008) *Testing times: The uses and abuses of assessment*. New York/London: Routledge.

Strauss, A., & Corbin, J. (1990) *Basics of qualitative research: Grounded theory procedures and techniques*. London: Sage.

Swain, H. (2012) 'Are lessons for lecturers the way ahead?'. *The Guardian* 20 November. Online: https://www.theguardian.com/higher-educationnet work/blog/2012/nov/20/lessons-for-lecturers-hea-roundtable (accessed 5 January 2013).

Telegraph, T. (2012) 'Alan Milburn: scrapping EMA was a 'very bad mistake', *The Telegraph* 18 October. Online: http://www.telegraph.co.uk/education/edu cationnews/9616615/Alan-Milburn-scrapping-EMA-was-a-very-bad-mis take.html(accessed 5 August 2015).

The Organization for Economic Cooperation and Development's (OECD) (2011) *Strong Performers and Successful Reformers in Education*: Education Policy Advice for Greece.

Thomas, E. (2001) *Widening Participation in Post-compulsory Education*. London: Continuum.

Tochluk, S. (2010) *Witnessing Whiteness: The Need to Talk About Race and How to Do It*. Maryland: Rowland and Littlefield Education.

Tooley, J., & Darby, D. (1998) *Educational Research, A Critique: a survey of published results*. London: Office of Standards in Education.

Tran, L. T., & Soejatminah, S. (2016) "Get foot in the door': International students' perceptions of work integrated learning' in *British Journal of Educational Studies*, Vol. 64 (3): 1–19.

Unterhalter, E., Ladwig, J., & Jeffrey, C. (2014) "Aspirations, education and social justice: applying Sen and Bourdieu' in British Journal of Sociology of Education, Vol. 35 (1): 133–145.

Vignoles, A., Goodman, A., Machin, S., & McNally, S. (2008) *Widening Participation in Higher Education: A Quantitative Analysis: Full Research Report ESRC End of Award Report, RES-139-25-0234.* Swindon: ESRC.

Vincent, C., & Ball, S. (2007) "Making up' the middle-class child: families, activities and class dispositions' in *Sociology*, Vol. 41 (6): 1061–1077.

Wadsworth, E., Dhillon, K., Shaw, C., Bhui, K., Stansfeld, S., & Smith, A. (2007) 'Racial discrimination, ethnicity and work stress' in *Occupational Medicine*, Vol. 57 (1): 18–24.

Walker, I., & Zhu, Y. (2011) 'Differences by degree: Evidence of the net financial rates of return to undergraduate study for England and Wales' in *Economics of Education Review*, Vol. 30 (6): 1177–1186.

Walkerdine, V. (1998) *Counting Girls Out: Studies in Mathematics Education.* London: Falmer Press.

Walsh, L. (2015) *Educating Generation Next: Young People, Teachers and Schooling in Transition.* Basingstoke: Palgrave MacMillan.

Watson, J. (2012) 'Butler's Biopolitics: Precarious Community' in *Theory and Event*, Vol. 15: 2.

Watt, P. (2009) 'Living in an oasis: middle-class disaffiliation and selective belonging in an English suburb' in *Environment & Planning*, Vol. 41 (12): 2874–2892.

Weiner, G. (1985) *Just a bunch of girls: feminist approaches to schooling.* Buckingham: Open University Press.

Welham, H. (2014) 'The glass ceiling in education: why are so few women becoming headteachers?' *The Guardian* 12 February. Online: https://www.theguardian.com/teacher-network/teacher-blog/2014/feb/12/women-headteachers-education-glass-ceiling-careers (accessed 1 May 2016).

Wilkins, A., & Burke, P. J. (2014) 'Widening participation in higher education: The role of professional and social class identities and commitments' in *British Journal of Sociology of Education*, Vol. 36 (3): 434–452.

Wilkins, S., Shams, F., & Huisman, J. (2013) 'The decision-making and changing behavioural dynamics of potential higher education students: the impacts of increasing tuition fees in England' in *Education Studies*, Vol. 39 (2): 125–141.

Wilkinson, R., & Pickett, K. (2010) *The Spirit Level: Why Equality is Better for Everyone.* London: Penguin.

Williams-Grut, T. (2015) 'France and Greece are dragging down European manufacturing'. 1 September. Online: http://uk.businessinsider.com/european-manufacturing-pmi-for-august-italy-spain-germany-2015-9 (accessed 17 November 2016).

Willis, P. (1977) *Learning to Labour: how working class kids get working class jobs.* Aldershot: Gower.

Woodrow, M., Foong Lee, M., McGrane, J., Osborne, B., Pudner, H., & Trotman, C. (1998) *From elitism to inclusion: Good practice in widening access to higher education* (main report). London: CVCP.

Wright, O. (2015) 'Key Government strategy in decline as apprenticeships fall'. *The Independent* 1 January. Online: http://www.independent.co.uk/news/uk/politics/key-government-strategy-in-decline-as-apprenticeships-fall-9953533.html (accessed 14 September 2016).

Yin, R. (1994) *Case study research: Design and methods.* London: Sage.

Young, I. M. (1990) *Justice and the Politics of Difference.* Princeton, NJ: Princeton University Press.

Zmas, A. (2014) 'Financial crisis and higher education policies in Greece: between intra- and supranational pressures' in *Higher Education*, Vol. 69 (3): 495–508.

INDEX

A

Apprenticeships, 19, 40–41, 44, 82–86, 109–113, 115, 121–124, 128–129, 132

Aspirations, 11–12, 14, 59, 62, 64–65, 68–72, 76, 80–82, 87–88, 93–94, 96–99, 101, 105, 107, 110, 126–128, 134–135

B

Bourdieu, Pierre, 11–14

C

Capital
 cultural, 11–14, 52, 106
 economic, 17, 52
 social, 12, 15, 49, 67, 94, 106, 115–116, 119, 123

Credentialisation, 2, 40, 86, 117, 119, 123

Dispositions, *see* Habitus

E

Educational Maintenance Allowance (EMA), 2–4, 26–28, 47–58, 77, 125–127

Ethnicity
 identity, 17, 99
 influence on employment, 2
 stereotypes, 16
 subject choices, 72–76, 100–102, 127

F

Field, *see* Habitus

G

Gender
 career pathway, 16, 127
 subject choices, 14–19, 59–66, 71, 76, 93, 95–99, 103, 127, 134

Gender as socially constructed, 6, 12–14, 49, 62–63
 See also Social constructionism

Graduate
 employment, 1–2, 5–6, 39, 83–84, 109, 111–112, 114–117, 126, 129, 135
 pressure to, 35, 129
 status, 39, 40, 113

© The Author(s) 2017
K. Hoskins, *Youth Identities, Education and Employment,*
Policy and Practice in the Classroom,
DOI 10.1057/978-1-137-35292-7

Lightning Source UK Ltd.
Milton Keynes UK
UKOW01n1442310717
306387UK00001B/87/P